MENAGERIE, 1

Pam Olink   1998

MENAGERIE, 1

Indonesian Fiction • Poetry • Photographs • Essays

John H. McGlynn, Editor

The Lontar Foundation, Jakarta

Manufactured in Indonesia.

Layout	:	Jessy Tansil (Tempo)
Design	:	Jessy Tansil & John H. McGlynn
Cover painting	:	*Labyrinth* (Original title: *Labirin*)
		by Dede Eri Supria, 1990
		Oil on canvas. 2 x 2 M
Cover photograph	:	Koko (Jakarta Program)
Typeface	:	Palatino, Helvetica Narrow
Typesetting	:	Retno Isti Pratiwi (Apple Mandiri)
Printer	:	PT Grafiti Pers & PT Intermasa

ISBN No. 979-8083-07-5

Acknowledgments

PUBLICATION OF *MENAGERIE, 1* would have not been possible without a substantial financial contribution from *TEMPO*. To this magazine, and especially to its management, we extend our fervent thanks.

Lontar would also like to thank the Indonesian authors for their literary contributions to *Menagerie, 1*, and the translators who have given Lontar so much of their valuable time. Further thanks must go to Jessy Tansil and Prinka of *Tempo* & *PT Graffiti Pers* for their freely-given assistance on the layout and design of this volume and other Lontar publications. Finally, we extend a note of thanks to Janet Boileau, of *Jakarta Program*, and to Karin Johnson, both of whom have frequently contributed their time and talents to Lontar.

Contents

More Stories

Editor's Note

WELCOME TO LONTAR'S MENAGERIE! Ever since the establishment of Lontar we have been searching for a format in which to present occasional translations of poems, short stories and literary essays. Because so few Indonesian authors have enough of their own work translated to warrant publication of individual titles -- and because we know that it might be years before they do -- we felt the need to come up with a forum in which to present the odd, one-off, translations of their works. *Menagerie* is the concept that we came up with: a series of volumes focusing on the Indonesian short story but also including poems and literary and photographic essays. *Menagerie, 1* is not, therefore, just an anthology of contemporary Indonesian literature. Rather, it is Lontar's first step towards the publication of a truly representative body of Indonesian literature in English.

    Menagerie, 1 was in part shaped by a request by Professor Robert Shapard of the University of Hawaii for a number of short stories to include in the Spring 1991 issue of *Manoa*. In the process of collecting stories for that University of Hawaii journal I collected translations of several dozen stories. After Professor Shapard had taken six, the question arose as to what to do with the rest? Such a relative abundance of translated Indonesian short stories decided us at Lontar to get on with our idea of publishing a journal-like volume of short stories. And thus — *Menagerie*.

Lontar's short-term goal of publishing *Menagerie* is, as previously mentioned, to provide an English-language forum for occasional translations of Indonesian literary pieces. The long-term goal of the *Menagerie* series is to bring into English enough translations of Indonesian short stories to permit publication of the first truly representative anthology of Indonesian short stories.

In 1956 John M. Echols published at Cornell University *Indonesian Writing in Translation*, a monograph containing translations of several Indonesian short stories. In 1968 Rufus Hendon published at Yale University a monograph entitled *Six Indonesian Short Stories*. Since that time other American and Australian universities have published collections of translations and Harry Aveling, arguably the most well known translator of Indonesian literature, has released several volumes of translations. But aside from the fact that most of these works are marred by faulty translations, none are representative of the wealth of short stories in the Indonesian language.

Whether a single book can ever claim to be "representative" is of course doubtful. Arthur Waley's two volume anthology of Chinese literature and Donald Keene's compendium of Japanese literature are both admirable works but neither can said to be truly representative. Is the *Norton Anthology of American Poetry* representative of American poetic styles? Can any one volume hope to represent the literary wealth of a culture? Almost certainly the answer must be a resounding no.

It is this knowledge of certain failure — the inability to produce a representative anthology — that strengthened our resolve to publish not just one anthology of short stories but a series of anthologies. Thus, we will not pretend that *Menagerie, 1* contains either the best Indonesian short stories ever written or stories by all of the best Indonesian writers. The same will be true for *Menagerie, 2* and for successive

Menageries. Perhaps in five or ten years, after the publication of fifteen or twenty volumes we might then be able to make the claim that a truly representative body of Indonesian literature is available in English, but not until that time.

Through *Menagerie* Lontar will present both the contemporary and the past, stories from the first part of this century as well as from the last. As the general editor of the *Menagerie* series it is my hope that readers will enjoy this process of gradual construction, this step-by-step fitting together of the jigsaw puzzle that is Indonesian literature. *Menagerie, 1* marks the start of a lengthy journey, one which I hope readers will enjoy and Lontar's financial sponsors will support. Contemporary Indonesian literature is the result of a centuries-old process. Let us not think that we can become well versed in Indonesian literature by the reading of just one or two volumes.

THE EDITOR

MENAGERIE, 1

Minem Has a Baby

KASDU KEPT WALKING. Moving away from the village, he took a narrow path that cut through the hills. To the right and left of the path rose steep cliffs where rocky earth lay in dry and brittle clumps. In the rainy season, this path became a riverbed through which water surged from the summit. Muddy water, cascading from above, had worn away the topsoil and had gradually carved the path deeper and deeper into the hill.

Exposed roots dangled from the steep banks like dead claws grabbing at the earth, which, eroded and eaten away, seemed to retreat, further and further from their grasp. Trees that had lost their footing leaned precariously and others had fallen entirely.

Kasdu's quick steps were accompanied by the crunching sound of dried leaves being crushed underfoot. The sun, which had been baking these hills for almost four months, was high in the sky, almost at its peak for the day. Its daily appearance had made the trees wilted and dry. Banana leaves bowed on their stalks. Stretches of tall weeds were the color of ash. Clumps of grass held in their roots the soil's last drops of water.

In the sunlight Kasdu's face looked hard. His eyebrows hid a stern gaze. His face showed the scars of harsh blows and he looked old — much older than his mere twenty years.

The hills on Kasdu's right and left were huge mounds of rock and limestone. Sere stumps and patches of weeds dotted the landscape. Dead trunks and branches jutting out of the ground completed the picture of desiccation. Some boys, their skin dry and ashen, were gathering twigs and branches for firewood. Others were digging the stony soil in search of what wild potatoes remained.

When thirst began to bite at Kasdu's throat, he suddenly realized that he had put nothing in his stomach since morning. He then recalled with relief that below the big *angsana* tree up ahead was a clear-water spring. He would relieve his thirst there, he thought as he quickened his pace.

Standing in front of the shallow hollow in the earth where the water usually collected, Kasdu stood dumbfounded. There wasn't a single drop of water. The hollow was full of dead *angsana* leaves. The tree itself was withered and almost leafless. Kasdu could do no more than swallow his own thick spittle and continue his long journey.

Slowly resuming his steps, he thought of his wife Minem. It was his fault that she now lay on her bed with a baby no bigger around than her arm sprawled feebly beside her. The infant was tiny, very tiny. Kasdu found it hard to believe that something that moved so weakly, a creature who seemed to mew like a kitten, could actually be a baby that would grow into a human being. It was even harder for him to imagine that the tiny infant was in fact his own flesh and blood.

Minem should not have given birth today, not just because she herself was only a child of fourteen, but also because she had only carried the child in her womb for seven months. So Kasdu's thoughts vexed him as he walked. Minem wouldn't have given birth for another two months if only I hadn't refused to fetch the water from across the village, he berated himself over and over again.

But the baby—no bigger around than one's arm—had been forced from Minem's womb after she had fallen while carrying a full jug of water. She had slipped on a steep bank and rolled down the slope. The earthenware jug had shattered, watering the parched earth. Minem, in a daze and with fluids from her womb dampening her batik skirt, had been led home by a passerby. The midwife who was called declared that the fetus had begun its descent. She was right, for a few hours later Minem gave birth to her first child—a tiny infant that cried like a kitten.

Kasdu himself had watched Minem lying on her back, her knees bent upright, her face bright red, and her breathing strained. Experienced women of the village stood by giving her advice during her labor, all the while mumbling prayers for her safety.

Kasdu felt sick at heart recalling how Minem had grimaced with pain, how she had held her breath, then contracted her stomach muscles to force the child out of her. After the infant emerged, Minem had lain motionless, her ghostly pale face drenched in sweat. She didn't move a muscle. Her weak pulse was the only sign that she was still alive. How *could* she still be alive when both she and her baby — such a tiny thing — looked so weak? Kasdu could not keep from his mind the nagging question of whether Minem and her child would survive.

Now Kasdu was on his way to his parents-in-law to tell them of what had happened. How they would react was a huge question that continued to confuse him. Would they be happy to be grandparents? Or would they be furious that Minem had given birth prematurely because he, her husband, had been unwilling to fetch some water from across the village? If it were the latter, Kasdu was done for. In his mind he could see his father-in-law's jaws growing rigid, looking as if they could crush a mountain between them. And he imagined the man's solid fist flying out at Kasdu's forehead.

No, he really didn't know. He didn't know what would happen. Just as he didn't know why his marriage to Minem had resulted in the birth of a baby so small. Just as he didn't know whether Minem and the baby were still alive at that moment. When he left her, Minem had looked so pitiful, so different from the fresh and lively woman she had been before. The child could only move weakly, curled up like a caterpillar stung by a wasp.

The closer he got to his father-in-law's, the slower Kasdu's pace became. Not just because he was tired, but even more because of the anxiety that began to creep into his heart. Once, he stopped in his tracks and stood as if dazed. He was tempted to turn back, for suddenly he felt unwilling to face his father-in-law, who would no doubt reproach him. But after a moment his doubts began to dissipate and his legs fall into step again.

His long journey under the beating sun came to an end when he entered his father-in-law's yard. Stopping for a moment to wipe the sweat from his forehead with the back of his hand, Kasdu pulled open the front door and called out a greeting, "*Kula nuwun.*"

Without waiting for a reply, he entered and sat down. He needed to calm his breathing. But his heart began to beat even faster. And he failed to hide his startled reaction when his father-in-law entered. His mother-in-law followed, a few steps behind, carrying a reddish infant in a sling around her shoulders.

"What are you doing here?" his father-in-law asked.

"Are you alone? Without Minem?" asked his mother-in-law.

"Yes, Ma, I came alone," Kasdu answered. His lips trembled. His mother-in-law noticed the worry come across his face.

"You're terribly pale, Kasdu. Are you sick?"

"No, Ma, I'm just thirsty."

"Wait a moment, I'll get you some water."

Even after drinking the glass of water Kasdu was still pale. He seemed nervous and frightened.

His father-in-law asked him gruffly, "Why are you here? Is it something important?"

"Yes, sir, it's important."

"If it's so important, why are you just standing there all flustered?"

"Well, sir . . . it's Minem."

"What about Minem?" his mother-in-law interrupted. "Is she sick?"

"No, Ma. Minem . . . uh, Minem had a baby. Minem's had her baby."

Kasdu waited uncertainly for his parents-in-law to react. He watched as they both stared at him with their mouths agape. For several moments they stood that way until, finally, his mother-in-law turned and spoke to her husband.

"Well, you're a grandfather now, and I'm a grandmother."

He seemed unimpressed with his wife's words.

"Just a minute, Kasdu. You mean to say Minem's already had a baby?"

"Yes, sir."

"Wait a minute. What did she have?"

"A baby, sir," Kasdu answered simply.

"Thing is, my wife just gave birth the day before yesterday. And my wife is twenty-nine years old, so it makes sense that she's having babies. But Minem's still a kid. Can a child give birth to a child? Good God! I can't believe Minem's had a baby. You sure it wasn't just a clot of blood or — heck! — maybe an egg or something?"

"Yes, I'm sure, sir. Minem's had a baby. But it's a really tiny thing because she was only seven months along," answered Kasdu, beginning to speak more easily. "And the baby is a girl."

The woman took her husband's hand. Kasdu could hear what she whispered to him. "What are you talking about, dear? Have you forgotten that I was only fourteen when Minem was born?"

"That's right, yes. But it still amazes me: not only a grown woman, but even a little girl can have a baby."

Who knows if Kasdu's father-in-law was amazed or not. But at that moment he smiled, remembering that in the next month he would have another occasion to celebrate in his house. This time it would be the marriage of Minah, Minem's twelve-year-old sister. "My girls are really popular," he said to himself. He was very proud.

1989

TRANSLATED BY ALAN FEINSTEIN

B. Y. TAND

Zero-Point

HE GAZES AT THE SUN and sees it spinning. He gazes at the moon and sees it spinning. He gazes at a stand of trees and sees them spinning. Looking inward, he sees himself spinning like a top. At zero-point the top topples. He examines the top. He examines its string but finds it tangled and knotted. He looks for the end of the string, searching carefully until he locates it, wound around and around a zero-point. Its strands, overlaid in multiple layers, form an oval and the oval surrounds a zero-point.

He gazes at Marni lying there, with her eyes shut. Beads of sweat stand on her brow, suggesting that she had just completed a difficult and exhausting task. He feels his own chest, also damp with sweat. Together they mounted a peak to sip from a spring of water as cool as a mountain lake. They bathed in sweat, swam and cavorted in a sea of their own perspiration. Now he watches Marni sleep, lost in her dreams. He gathers her wrap of batik cloth that had been cast to the side of the bed when they began their ascent, then slowly drapes it over her body. For a moment his hand pauses in mid-air before he finally draws back the cloth again. He studies her body's entirety. Such exquisitely smooth skin. Her waist-length hair makes her appear so feminine.

He hastens to kill the doubt that flares suddenly in his mind, fearing that doubt, like the string of a top, might bind him even tighter. He could then be spun and would spin until he arrived back at the zero-point. It is the zero-point that precipitated this conflict, he says to himself. He kisses Marni's brow deeply, so deeply that he founders in the depths of his soul. He then covers Marni again, drawing the cloth upward as far as her breasts. At that moment she begins to stir. She stretches. Her eyes open to seek his eyes. Their eyes meet, a spark kindles. And Marni cuddles up to him, a coy embrace.

"Was it good?"

"Yes, and you?"

"Hmmm, yes. You're were like a wild stallion trampling the Sumbawa plains."

"Marni..."

"Yes?"

The man doesn't continue his thought. He feels like a top spinning inside a circle. He looks into the woman's eyes, deeply, as if searching for something there. Her eyes, with a light as cool as the mountain lake from which they have just drunk, are colored with tenderness and love. The eyes of a woman no different from the eyes of other women. Eyes that seek in a man, protection.

"Why are you so quiet? Say what's on your mind. Are you hungry?"

Marni presses her breasts to his chest. She strokes his chest, so very softly that he is almost consumed again. But he climbs up from the zero-point, breaking through the dense jungle. Hurriedly he pours the remnants of his love onto the ground to let it crawl off in search of a new vessel.

He searches his heart to see if it is truly empty now. His eyes squeezed shut, his lips move as if to say something to Marni. But before any words can escape his mouth, Marni bends and kisses his breast. A coolness penetrates him to his marrow. Her hand massages the nape of his neck as she whispers something that she has often whispered in his ear in moments preceding their ascents. The man looks into Marni's eyes and smiles, burrowing into the gentleness there. His quarrying ceases when Marni suddenly shuts her eyes and simultaneously parts her moist lips. He is at once flung into an ancient well of crystal water. Looking at his reflection in the water he sees that he is a whole man again, that the vessel is full once more.

He gazes at the sun and sees it spinning. He gazes at the moon and sees it spinning. Looking inward he sees himself spinning like a top. At zero-point the top topples. He examines the top. He looks at his wife and sees her spinning. He looks at his children and finds them spinning, too. But, finally, everything stops at the zero-point. It is intolerable to think of leaving again, to roll, to spin, to return to the zero-point. Stars hang before his eyes, a swarm around his pupils, dancing, singing, turning this way and that. As if something has caused his chest to constrict, his breath grows labored.

His voice is horse, his eyes are shut tight. "Do you agree?" he asks.

Marni doesn't answer. A damn has burst to inundate the flowers in the garden. She had long suspected that one day this man would say these words for he, this man, her husband, has another woman, his first wife. As the flood waters recede, only flower stems and sopping leaves remain. The flower pots are broken. The soil has been washed away, perhaps to a nameless sea.

Marni composes herself. Although she is screaming inside, she knows that she must face the inevitable. She kisses the man's forehead, a long and slow kiss. He presses shut his eyelids to stave off the movement of a point that has begun to move slowly away from the zero-point.

"Do you need my assent? Isn't it you who must decide? As the man, don't you hold the key to the marriage? I've always thought that you might come to that decision. I am powerless."

"Even if it is a right that has been conferred on me, and one to which I have given my assent, on the basis of a social contract, I do not want to decide alone. I want this to be a joint decision. You too have just as much right as I to argue why we must part."

The woman feels as if she is about to choke. Suddenly she feels that she is hanging from the sky with no rope, but is too dizzy and too frightened to jump down. Were she to try to climb up, her hands would never reach the firmament's base. Her head begins to spin when she sees the sharp rocks waiting to greet her fall.

"I know you love me with all your heart. But I know you love your wife and children, too. You can't divide your love evenly, can you?"

"No..."

"Who do you love more?"

"You!"

"And her?"

"The same as you."

Marni laughs. The man laughs too. The walls of the room laugh. The gecko lizards, too. The entire scene dissolves in a fit of laughter.

"Are you saying that you can divide your love into three equal parts?"

"Yes."

"With one of the thirds for me?"

"Yes."

"And one third for your first wife?"

"Yes."

"And one third for your children?"

"Yes."

"Have you ever asked your first wife's permission to leave her? Have you ever heard her arguments?"

"No."

"Why?"

"Have you?"

"No."

"Why?"

The woman shakes her head. Her eyes fill with tears, glimmering crystalline. Like jewels, a million sparks glittering on their facets. The man shook his head. His eyes filled with tears, they too glimmering crystalline. Like jewels, a million sparks glittering on their facets. The zero-point falls on their chests. To mingle with his male sweat. To mingle with her female sweat. The zero-point falls into his wife's womb, issued from a pistol fired a previous night. The zero-point falls into Marni's womb, issued from a pistol fired this afternoon.

1982

TRANSLATED BY T.E. BEHREND

Orez

OREZ HAD NOT LIVED all that long. He was only five years and three months old. But because of him my wife and I had changed jobs frequently and moved eight times.

Even before my marriage there had been omens of my future family's misfortune.

Hester Price, the woman who would become my wife, told me that she would go anywhere I wanted to go and do whatever I wanted to do. But when I spoke of my plans to marry her, she reacted with shock and terror. She screamed and, trying to stifle her cry, clamped her lower lip with her teeth. She grabbed her throat so tightly that her eyes almost popped out of their sockets.

Later, in the evening of that same day, she telephoned to offer an apology. She said that she was deeply grateful for my desire to marry her and that she loved me and respected me. But, she also said, a woman like her would not make me a proper wife. With great sincerity she suggested that I find someone else, a woman who would be better for me. When I urged her to explain why, she refused.

After a long, involved process she finally consented to speak to her father. I hadn't thought that her father would be all that old, but the look in his eyes, his gloomy face and wrinkled skin convinced me that he was ready to be mummified, that he had lived far too long. I suspected that he might disintegrate if he were not immediately preserved. His features indicated that his life had not been a pleasant one. Every hardship he experienced had etched another wrinkle on his face. The way he held his pipe indicated that even though tobacco disgusted him, he could not stop smoking, that he had enslaved himself to smoking in order to forget a life that was for him one misery after another.

The old man, Stevick Price, Hester's father, appeared ready to talk to me when I introduced myself as a friend of his daughter's. He told me to sit down, then asked if I wouldn't have some coffee.

While Hester was making the coffee, Stevick gave me a look I could only construe as pity. He then asked if it were true that I wanted to marry his daughter. When I said "yes," he asked whether I had thought out the matter thoroughly. When I said "yes," he asked me if I loved his daughter. When I said "yes," he said that he was deeply grateful for that, but added that I might come to regret it.

It was then that Stevick got to the heart of the problem. He said he had forgotten how many children he had fathered — maybe it was seven, maybe eight, or maybe as many as nine — but that all of them, except for Hester, had died because of birth defects. Some had been born without arms or legs, one had had an oversized head, another's head had been on backwards, and so on. He was worried that Hester might share the same fate as her mother. He explained that Hester's mother had died a long time ago, not out of sorrow, but out of despair and shame.

He could not say what would happen if Hester were to have children but, even so, he wanted me to nurse the question a thousand times over before I came to a decision. At this point his eyes misted over and as soon as Hester entered the room with the coffee, he excused himself to return to his room. "Excuse me, young man, I can't keep you company very long. I've said what I needed to say. The rest is up to you."

Hester looked at me then immediately looked away, avoiding my eyes as if from shame or self-disgust. But seeing her, my pulse raced with my desire for her. I took her hand and asked her to join me for a walk in the woods behind the university's Union Building.

I felt like an animal and knew that I would treat Hester like one if I were alone with her. I clutched her hand, my arm securely fastened around her waist. The muscles of my legs twitched with the desire to meld into her, for my body to become an extension of hers, my hands her own.

The fragrance of trees and grass along Fess Street heightened my desire. Upon nearing a small river, the Jordan River it was called locally, I felt that my mind was made up. Everything was clear. I looked at the river and noticed its strange color. While the tributary to the river that joined the larger course some distance from Union Building ran clear, the stream that flowed beside the building was turbid. At the confluence of the two streams, the river was a muddy color and void of clarity. I stood there for quite some time. Hester seemed to understand I was thinking about something; her hand was moist with cold sweat. I pulled her into the woods. And in those woods two animals became aware of themselves as beasts and treated one another as such.

A month after I married Hester she was already showing signs of pregnancy. Three months later her stomach had gained in girth. And the larger her abdomen became, the more apprehensive she appeared. She was frequently anxious and had trouble sleeping. At times she cried out in her sleep for no reason at all.

As Hester grew larger, her father grew thinner and weaker until he fell ill. But before the doctor ordered him into the hospital, the old man asked me several times to come and see him. He spoke to me slowly at these meetings, in a heavy but faint voice I had difficulty hearing.

Over and over again he told me how glad he was that I had married

Hester. But time and again he demanded that I be a responsible husband, as if fearing that I might start to abuse her. "I don't need to explain what I mean by `responsibility'," he said. "You, as her husband, young man, should already know what I mean."

Often, too, he would remind me that even though Hester's life and death were in God's hands, I had the power to hasten or hinder the pace at which her death would come. He repeatedly told me to take the best possible care of Hester: "Love her life as you love your own, and care for her body as you would your own."

From these sessions I learned that Hester and I were, for him, more important than any children we might have, that is if our children were born abnormal. As for our future offspring, he advised that I let live those who could have a good life but not force life on those who would find it difficult. Apparently he had no objection to my neglecting our children if they were born with defects, as long as one were sure that they, like Hester's siblings, would not live long, and that in living their lives would cause Hester and me much suffering.

When Stevick died, neither Hester nor I felt much emotion; we felt neither relief nor sorrow. It was time for him to die; there was no purpose in a continued life. His life had been one of great suffering. He had found pleasure in seeing Hester become my wife but had become apprehensive when Hester became pregnant, not knowing what the outcome would be for the unborn child. Whatever happened to the child, he left to Hester and me. He was certain of my sense of responsibility and with that certainty he had calmly departed this life. Hester and I prayed God would receive his soul. We also prayed that the child Hester carried would be good, happy, and of noble character. Amen.

Hester decided to sell Stevick's ramshackle house before it collapsed on its own. We sold it at a low price to the Bill Morrow Real Estate Agency without bothering to remove the furniture. We gave his clothes away to Opportunity House, a charity, for the use of anyone who needed them. I disposed of his car, which was almost as far gone as Stevick himself, at the junk yard on the city's edge after the advertisement that I ran drew no response. I had wanted to set aside his pipe for myself but because of business matters that kept me constantly occupied, I soon forgot where he had stored the pipe. I regretted not having it, but there was nothing I could do and I never saw the pipe again.

My regret about the loss of Stevick's pipe was immediately forgotten when I found in his house a sword stored neatly in a long case. While the sword had not been properly looked after, it was still shiny and in fairly good condition. Its sheath, however, was threadbare and drenched in the musty smell of a jacket that had hung unworn too long in a dark closet. Hester knew little about the sword's history. She said that it might have belonged to the great-grandfather of a friend of her father's. If she weren't wrong, she said, her father's friend's ancestor had found the sword beside a dead Yankee soldier on the Kentucky border near the end of the Civil War. She wasn't certain, however, and just how the sword had come to be in her father's possession she knew nothing at all. What she did remember, quite clearly, was that one day her father, angry for no apparent reason, had run out of the family house, sword in hand, and furiously hacked away at any tree he had come across. That's all Hester remembered; that's how her father had used the sword. Hester said that if she were not mistaken, her father's bout of strange behavior had occurred after the birth of one of her brothers, possibly Jason, who had died only a few months after birth.

Without a word passing between us, Hester and I came to the understanding I would ask nothing about her pregnancy. The name of her doctor, her schedule of appointments, what her doctor said, and what kinds of medicines her doctor prescribed, if her doctor prescribed any at all, were items of information not discussed with me. I knew that she was afraid to talk about her pregnancy, and she knew well enough that I would not be enthusiastic were I to hear that anything was going wrong. But because I had to sign the necessary insurance papers, I did in fact come to know which doctor she saw, when she saw her, and how much her medical examinations and prescriptions cost. Hester never gave the insurance papers directly to me. She left them in a drawer near the lamp. I retrieved them from there, signed them, and sent them to the insurance company in St. Louis.

Hester's anxiousness increased steadily. One day, she admitted that her friends at work were very patient with her and were always excusing her for the mistakes she made. But the more errors she made, the worse she felt, and because of this she was considering changing jobs. I forbade this but in the days that followed she told me that her anxiety was so great that her mistakes were piling up, mountain high. "Hold on a while longer," I told her. "Try to stay calm," I advised. But eventually her fears affected me and even I could find no peace. Regardless, every time we touched, our desire for each other flared. This passion, to be sure, was the passion of animals but we made love ever more frequently, as if our lives depended on it.

Finally, one day I received a call from the hospital. Hester had gone straight to the hospital from work having had no chance to come home first. She was hemorrhaging, the nurse who called told me. When I asked if Hester wanted me to be there, she said that Hester was barely conscious and so I should come. I left immediately.

When seeing Hester we avoided looking into each other's eyes, but I was sure that she, like me, longed to touch and to ignite the animal lust that had become our spirit for life.

The baby, our first, was pronounced dead. What the baby looked like, whether it was whole or not, or anything else, I was afraid to ask. And Hester prevented the doctor and her staff from telling me.

Our second baby met the same fate, as did our third. After that Hester and I agreed not to hope for any more children. Instead we cultivated our wild and free animal lust. Without saying so verbally, we both reminded each other that life was not just hell, that there was a heaven beyond, that we could share. This was the pact that bound us unspoken and which we affirmed with actions.

Quite unexpectedly, Hester became pregnant again. This time her abdomen looked different. The sides of her stomach curved but her skin seemed exceptionally tough, as if made from the leather of a soccer ball. While in her previous pregnancies her belly was like a hill with sloping sides, this time, though it was only the first trimester, it extended outward like Krakatau Volcano before its eruption hundreds of years ago.

Hester told me she wanted an abortion but I did not agree. She understood my feelings, she said, and knew that I too was suffering but it was she alone who had to suffer physically. I might be able to empathize, she told me, but I could never really know what it was like. I could not argue and, in the end, all I could say was, "It's up to you."

Hester's plan for an abortion failed because under Indiana state law abortion was viewed as a heinous crime. Hester considered going to Kentucky but the laws there were just the same. This was true of Ohio as well.

On her own, Hester flew to Chicago. According to the information she had received, even though Illinois outlawed abortion, in certain cities like Chicago and Peoria there were several doctors who had the authority to perform an abortion as long as there were justifiable health, religious, or moral reasons. Regardless, she came home still pregnant. She did not tell me why, and I was not one to ask. To myself I blamed her only for not telephoning Chicago first before wasting time and money flying there.

Hester took to locking herself in the bathroom for long periods of time. This I wouldn't have objected to as long as what she was doing was not harmful, but the sounds emanating from the bathroom made me grow suspicious.

My suspicions were confirmed when I peeked inside. She was jumping from the floor onto the sink counter, from there to the toilet, then to the edge of the bathtub and back to the floor before starting all over again. I tried to ignore her but in the end I could not bear it. And when she refused to stop and to open the door, I was forced to break the door down.

She fell sobbing into my arms. She told me it was all her fault and asked me to forgive her. She said she loved me and was grateful, not just because I had married her, but also because of my unwillingness to divorce her. Then we became animals again.

The baby had no desire to leave Hester's womb; in fact it grew ever larger. And the larger Hester's belly grew the more pronounced her anxiety became.

One night Hester stared into space for the longest time. She seemed to be thinking about something but I didn't have the nerve to ask what it was. Finally, however, she confessed to me that earlier in the afternoon after her lunch break, she had been late returning to work because she had become preoccupied watching a group of small children playing baseball at Dunn Field. She said she had paid close attention to how the children put on their mitts and then threw the ball with their free hand. She studied how they threw the ball toward the batter and how the batter hit the ball as hard as possible. She noticed how the ball was propelled into the air with impressive force. "What if," she then asked, "a pregnant woman were walking by when the children were playing ball and the bat accidently hit the woman in the stomach? What do you think would happen?"

Her question made me shudder but I said nothing. She stared at me for some time, waiting for an answer. "Okay," she then said, "it wouldn't have to be the bat that hits her in the stomach but supposing the ball, travelling as fast as it does, were to hit her. What do you think would happen?" I shuddered again. She then began to cry but soon got a grip on herself and, in one swift move, jumped up from the bed and quickly removed some clothes. Pointing her belly towards me she ordered me to punch it like a boxer would in trying to knock out an opponent. I refused. She repeated the order, this time in a louder, more demanding, voice. But still I refused.

She dragged me into the living room and, after removing the rest of her clothes, lay down on the floor sideways, her stomach pointing outwards, towards me. Then, like a referee without a whistle, she ordered me to kick her belly like a soccer ball. "Kick me like you were shooting a penalty goal," she commanded. I refused. Her tone slackened into a pleading whine. I refused.

She was disappointed at my stubbornness, she said, and then shifted her position. This time her belly faced the ceiling. She told me to use her stomach like a jumpoff mark for the long jump. She ordered me to move back away from her, take a short run and jump from her stomach to the window sill. I again refused. She begged me to mount her belly and ride it like a wild bronco. She told me that if anything happened the blame would all be hers. I wasn't certain what she meant by that.

And I didn't find out until the next day when, searching for a pencil in a drawer, I found a letter written by Hester and addressed to whomever found it. In the letter she said that at the time of its writing she was healthy, of clear mind, and under no untoward pressure, that she was writing the letter of her own volition and without coercion from anyone.

After stating that she loved, respected, and held in esteem her husband, she then explained her desire that her husband beat, hit, and step on her abdomen until the child she was carrying miscarried. With this statement, she wrote, she hoped that anything that happened would be considered her responsibility. In order to assure herself that the letter would not be missed and go unread, "I have written several letters like this and put them in different places," she explained where the letters could be found, two of which were at her office.

That night we agreed not to discuss the matter anymore. Life was not just hell, we confirmed, that in each others' bodies we knew there was something other than hell. After that we shared in an orgy of ecstasy to further convince ourselves. We then promised to let her belly be and that whatever happened would be Hester's business.

Hester said nothing more until around the time the baby Hester later named Orez was due. And then she only told me that it was about time to get ready. She had prepared a small bag of things to take to the hospital when the time came. Inside were clothes she would need, as well as things for Orez. I could tell from her behavior that she would be a good mother. But before I could compliment her she beat me to it, saying that I would surely be a good, responsible father. The way she said "responsible" reminded me of her dead father. I also remembered her father's instructions that I give priority to the comfort, happiness, and welfare of those who lived and had hope of a good life, and to forget those who passed away and those who could not live a happy life. His advice was a reflection of his own life, during which he had loved Hester and tried to forget his other children and also his wife, who had died and left him behind.

One evening around five o'clock, Hester told me she was having abdominal pains. I telephoned her doctor immediately. Her office closed at five, but luckily she was willing to take the call. She asked if Hester had discharged fluid, mucus, or blood. I told her she hadn't. In that case, she told me, just let things run their course and that as soon as Hester discharged any kind of fluid, bring her to the hospital immediately. I hung up and ran down to the parking lot to check on the car again. I had already checked it several times before but I had to check it again. Yes, I did want to be a good father or, perhaps more accurately, a responsible one.

In the middle of the night Hester discharged mucus. Not more than a few seconds later we were standing by the bank of elevators. The elevator on the right was apparently out of order, while the light of the elevator on the left indicated that it was parked on the fifth floor. We lived on the twelfth floor! Because there was no place to sit, Hester was forced to stand, leaning against me. This time our nearness gave rise not to lust but to a shared sense of responsibility. I felt strong. My body had the strength of a thousand-headed giant; my will was that of a charismatic leader who never lost an election; my mind was as clear as water; my legs, I felt, were as tall as pine trees. From the look in Hester's eyes I knew that she was trying to tell me that her life was in my hands. In my gaze I responded that I would do whatever my instincts dictated to safeguard the life she had entrusted to me.

The elevator was still on the fifth floor. As it was impossible to expect Hester to navigate the emergency stairs, I had to leave her leaning against a pillar while I ran down the stairs to the fifth floor. By the time I got there the elevator had already descended to the ground floor, but one glance at the furniture stacked outside the elevator told me that someone was moving. The elevator was out of general use because someone was monopolizing it to move their things. I rushed down to the first floor, fortunately to find the person moving still busy with his things. He had locked the elevator to make sure it stayed on first. After I pointedly told him my predicament, he apologized and sped with me back up to the twelfth floor. Hester looked more dead than alive by the time we got there. All the blood seemed to have drained from her face. The mover grabbed her bag while I picked Hester up from the floor. The mover went with us to the car and saw Hester safely inside.

I raced out of the parking lot onto Red Bud Hill Street, then down Everman and safely onto Campus View Drive without incident. Then I saw that we were in big trouble ahead. The light at the railroad crossing was flashing red. In only a few seconds a warning bell would signal the imminent passage of a freight train. I was right. A split second later the automatic bell sounded: "Ding-dong-ding, ding-dong-ding, ding-dong-ding..." The freight trains that passed through the city usually had lots of cars, sometimes up to two hundred. Because regulations forced freight trains to slow down when passing through the area, I knew that if I waited we would lose a lot of precious time. I remembered that three days before, the newspaper, television, and radio had carried the story of a man in his twenties who had been hit and killed by a train when his car stalled on the tracks not more than five blocks from where I was. The train was coming closer. From the look in Hester's eyes I knew that any decision was in my hands. If I wanted to risk a collision she wouldn't object; if I wanted to wait and let the baby be born in the car, before we reached the hospital, that was fine too. The rattling of the train grew louder, its light, brighter. Suddenly it occurred to me that I was young and strong and that even if the car were to stall I could pull Hester safely to the other side of the tracks. I also knew the car was in perfect condition. With impressive speed the car leapt forward to the other side of the tracks. Hester was safe; the baby in her womb, the car, and I were safe. In a flash the car was on South Tenth, then Fess, then Grant, and then racing down South Seventh to West Second until finally we reached the emergency entrance at the hospital. Before I jumped from the car I noticed blood flooding the seat beneath Hester. And no sooner had Hester been stretched out in emergency obstetrics than Orez was born. His cries carried the force of an earthquake. The earth shook, hospital walls cracked and shutters fell from their hinges.

Indeed, Orez survived, but he was deformed. His head was misshapen, lumpy, and far too large for his body. He might very well grow fangs, like a giant, someday. His hands and feet were also large, but his body was small. And every time he cried it felt like an earthquake rocking the city. He would have amazing strength, that boy, greater than that of a wild buffalo.

Day by day Orez' cries became louder and his strength grew. Our neighbors treated us kindly. They knew Orez was deformed. Although we were sure they were disturbed by Orez' crying, they never complained and always remained friendly towards us. They never showed any disgust at Orez and never forbade their children to go near him.

Both Hester's colleagues and mine treated us decently. They knew Orez was deformed, but they never talked about it. The few who saw Orez showed no abhorrence either. They treated him nicely. We were often invited with Orez to their homes for dinner. We knew that they were sincere and well-meaning in their treatment of us, and of Orez, but we were ashamed. Eventually Hester changed jobs, as did I, several times. We changed apartments frequently as well.

As his age increased it became clear that Orez' deformity extended beyond his body and his voice. His behavior was abnormal as well. Often, and for no reason at all, he would scream like Tarzan of the Jungle calling his beasts. It didn't matter whether it was day or night; when something bothered him, he screamed. And every time he screamed earthquakes shook the city to its most distant suburbs. All he ever said was, "Ham...hem...ham..." and growled like a yawning lion.

Orez could leap impressive lengths and heights. He loved to jump. When riding the elevator, for example, he would leap out each time the doors opened — unfortunately, without looking right or left — and sometimes before the doors were completely open. When his body struck the doors it was with earthquake force and the sound of thunder. When he collided with people waiting for the elevator they were jolted up and down.

Whenever he was playing, kicking a ball on the playground, onlookers could not help but be impressed by his unusual strength. The problem was that he couldn't aim. If by chance he got a proper fix, the ball would fly to seventh heaven. But if his legs were poorly positioned, he too would go flying into the air.

He also behaved strangely at meal times. He did not like to sit down on a chair but would instead run rapidly around the table, sometimes screaming with terrifying force. And he never bothered to check if what was on the table was something he liked to eat. If his flying fingers grabbed a hamburger, he gulped down the hamburger. If he happened to grab a sandwich, that was what he crammed into his mouth. He ate

27

like a pig — rapidly, smacking his lips with relish.

But when Orez was quiet, he was as quiet as Dracula asleep in his coffin.

Out of embarrassment Hester drifted from one job to another. I did the same. We moved from one apartment to another. And on and on and on. Because we had little savings and never lived in one neighborhood for very long, we chose not to buy a house.

About a week after we had moved to the Gourley Pike Apartments, we were watching a boxing match one day between champion boxers from Louisville and Detroit. The two men fought with great dexterity, both hard-hitting and demonstrating impressive footwork as well. Orez copied them move for move, as heated as if he wished to kill his shadow opponent, as if fighting for his own life. And just as the Louisville fighter slugged the boxer from Detroit in the nose, Orez leapt toward the table and struck it a mighty blow. The table rocked, upsetting the glasses and plates and causing them to fall to the floor.

Orez howled as if he himself were in pain. But when I shut off the TV he became furious and demanded that I turn it on again. I chose another channel, but he would have none of that. On and on he hollered until I finally gave in and switched the television back to the original channel. Now the Detroit champ was pummeling his Louisville opponent as if he wanted to murder him. Orez became even more excited at imitating the boxers. Just as the Louisville champ picked himself up off the mat and threw a punch at the Detroit fighter's nose, someone knocked on our door. I started to get up to answer it, but Orez beat me to it. With incredible speed he raced to the door and with one turn of the knob had it open. Before our guest could say a word, Orez attacked her viciously, as if he himself were the Louisville champ out to avenge himself on the Detroit fighter. Our guest fell to the floor with a thud, her cosmetics samples scattering everywhere. With a deafening scream Orez butted her then smashed his fist into her mouth and nose and chin over and over again. Hester and I had difficulty pulling

Orez off of his victim but finally we succeeded. Afterwards we apologized to Janet Tumblin, the cosmetics dealer, who seemed willing to overlook her bleeding nose and swollen lip. To further calm her nerves we bought all the cosmetics she had with her, even though we didn't need them.

Orez' attack on Janet Tumblin opened a new chapter in our lives. Hester, as if feeling ashamed and at fault, would shrink in fear each time I approached. My very proximity made her anxious. She acted just like she did when I had asked her to marry me. I felt sorry for her. I wanted to be close to her and to make her understand that I held nothing against her, that she had done nothing to hurt me, but because she seemed to fear me so, I kept my distance. I was afraid that if I kept pressing myself on her I would only make her suffer more.

Before Hester's fear began to thaw and I was able to come close to her again, I felt unbearably lonely. I took long walks around Union Building and spent hours staring at the water where the clear and the turbid tributaries met in the Jordan River. For a reason that was never clear to me I sometimes visited Stevick's grave.

Orez did not improve.

Eventually things did change. Hester began to show signs that she would not refuse my attention. Then, one night, she told me how much she loved me and how grateful she was that I still wanted her as my wife. She admitted that she had been watching me when, during the previous few days, I had taken out her father's sword and played with it, a habit I had developed. "If there's ever an accident because of that sword," she told me, "I'll take full responsibility." She also told me she knew that I kept the sword in the trunk of my car.

One day, for no reason it seemed, Orez went berserk. He growled, roared, howled, screamed, threw furniture around, butted into this and that. On and on. Hester couldn't stop him no matter how hard she tried and finally she broke down in tears. Then, like a ravenous lion, Orez roared and leapt at me. There was an evil look in his eyes. I retreated but he followed. I blocked his attack but he countered even more fiercely. Glasses and dishes crashed to the floor in violent disarray. Then, suddenly and without warning, he stopped all on his own. From his steady breathing I knew he wasn't all that tired. Maybe he just wanted to take a break. He then approached me, laughing, as if he had completely forgotten all that had gone before. When I stroked his hair he laid his head on my lap, as if asking me to love him. When I asked him if he would like to go outside he laughed happily and nodded, sounding his pleasure, "hhhhrrr... gggrrr... khkhkhrrr..." But when Hester was changing his clothes he rebelled. He wanted her to dress him in his very best clothes. Orez laughed with pleasure when she finally consented. Although he was deformed Orez looked well-groomed in those clothes. He looked noble, like a priest about to lead a solemn ritual. Orez seemed proud of his mother's skill in sewing garments that suited him and took pleasure in the fact that the clothes she made fit him so well. But then, when Hester began to change her clothes, he went berserk again. He pushed Hester, who nearly fell and then he butted me again and again. I tried to explain that Hester wanted to go with us, but he would have nothing to do with it. Again, Hester and I gave in. When she saw us to the door her eyes shone with tears.

Orez and I waited for the elevator quite some time. While we were waiting some kids who were heading downstairs from the 10th floor gathered in a circle around Orez. Because it was Saturday and they had no school, there was quite a bunch of them. When they laughed Orez laughed, and when he laughed they laughed even louder. The encounter became a competition to see who could laugh the loudest. Even when laughing in unison, however, those kids could not outdo Orez. His laughter was much louder and higher than theirs. Then they clapped their hands, applauding his voice. Orez clapped too.

At that point the elevator opened. There were already a few people inside, including two or three children. Without a starting run Orez jumped toward the open doors and, though it quite some distance, landed right on the spot. This was the first demonstration at Gourley Pike Apartments of his prowess at jumping. Everyone was duly impressed, and the children clapped their hands in delight. The elevator stopped again on the ninth floor. Some people tried to get on but were checked by Orez who suddenly leapt out at them. His leap took him quite a ways. The adults were silent with astonishment even as the children cheered. When the elevator stopped on the seventh floor, Orez leapt out again, this time slamming into somebody trying to get in. Both fell down, head first. On and on this way. Orez lacked no number of witnesses to his behavior that day.

When leaving the building Orez gripped my hand tightly, something he didn't often do. When we got into the car he insisted on sitting on my lap. This too was not ordinary. And when we stopped at some vending machines to buy snacks and a couple of Cokes, he held onto me with all his might, as if afraid that I would leave him behind. Most often he ran around at high speed, scrambling here and there, making it almost impossible to catch him. These changes in behavior were sometimes sudden, sometimes gradual, but the motivation behind them was never really clear.

What happened next was out of my hands. Though I held the steering wheel, Orez decided where to go. When I wanted to turn onto Indiana Avenue he pointed to the left, so I turned left. When we entered Dunn Street he pointed to the right, so I went right. This continued until, in the end, the car passed the site of the former Stevick place. The old house had disappeared long ago, replaced by a grey wooden structure with an oversized chimney. I stopped for a moment and Orez gazed at it with a bright face. He then ordered me to move on. So we left with me steering the car in whatever direction he willed.

Eventually we left the city and came to a somewhat isolated area. There, at the edge of a woods, Orez demanded that I stop the car. He then leapt from the vehicle and ran away from me, scurrying round the winding paths. Then he returned and led me away by the hand.

The weather was beautiful, the trees and grass fragrant, but my feet felt too heavy to drag very far. Orez seemed to feel the same. From the way he held my hand I could tell he wanted to go back. Suddenly the wind picked up, setting the trees to dancing and Hester's story about how her father had hacked down the trees with his sword flashed to mind.

I returned to the car, but not to leave. I opened the trunk and, trembling, took out the thin, elongated case that held Stevick's sword. Orez watched me. We then headed back down one of the paths towards the woods, Orez' hand in mine. He seemed to want to go home but this time I was determined to set the course.

I clutched his arm as we entered the woods. When we came to a small clearing he began to protest but I succeeded in getting him under control. He consented to stay with me when I told him to sit down beside a stone. He didn't resist when I placed his head on the stone, but he refused to lie face downwards. Maybe he wanted to look at the sky overhead. When I opened the case he was laughing, his eyes on the sky, skimming the tips of the trees that encircled the clearing. Just as I took out the sword he looked my way. I forced him to roll over but he refused to stay put. Finally I gave up and let him watch me. When I drew the sword from its sheath his eyes widened. Once more I tried to persuade him to roll over, but he would have none of it. When the sword slipped free of the sheath Orez laughed but then, when I swung the sword towards his neck, he leapt away, screaming in terror. I too was afraid. Cold sweat bathed my body, not only from fear, but remorse. I knew I was no prophet, because Orez had not surrendered himself or turned into a lamb. Instead, he had run away and remained what he was: Orez. The trees did not transform to holy men to bow before me or offer me hymns. I was no more than a beast. Hester too.

On the way back to the car, Orez decided to wander. Near a fork in the path I came across the remains of a camp fire. There were a number of empty cans, some papers and a few magazines and newspapers. Someone had probably camped there the night before. Because I had not read the paper in a while, and they looked fairly recent, I picked one up. The first thing to catch my eye was a photo of the Red Valley Creek in southern Indiana, a river that cut through a gorge near a rest area not far from Martinsville. According to the paper the river had claimed five victims in the last two weeks. All of them had slipped from the steep banks into the water and been carried away by the swift current and drowned. I threw away the paper and decided I would go there. But the way Orez was acting made it quite clear that he wanted to go home. He had no idea what I really wanted to do. I had witnesses to his behavior. People had seen how he jumped here and there without ever looking where he was going. If anything happened to Orez the verdict would be accident.

As the car neared Martinsville I became frightened. Orez had never asked to be born. Because of that, he had a right to live. I knew that if he could possibly use reason, he would never want to live with his deformities. But because he was deformed, nobody could change the way he was. Although his mind was dull and much of his behavior irrational, it is unlikely that he would jump off the bank and let himself be washed away in the creek. Like me, he knew fear, and he would do whatever he could to protect himself. Also like me he did not want to come to any harm. In the end, I decided to go home.

As soon as we entered the Gourley Pike parking lot, Orez jumped from the car and ran toward the entrance to the building. Several small children saw him and chased after him but none of them could catch up with him. He stopped at the building's entrance. The children surrounded him. Some of them had seen his skill in leaping from the elevator. The oldest child of the group, whose name was Norman, asked me if it would be all right if he and his friends asked Orez to play. I gave my permission and told them to call me if anything happened. It turned out that Norman and his friends already knew my apartment number. Without my being aware, I was famous among the kids as Orez' father. They knew exactly where I lived.

I returned to the apartment alone. When I opened the door Hester looked at me inquiringly. We held each other in a long embrace, then changed again to beasts. "Where's Orez?" she finally asked. I led her to the window, hoping that we would be able to see Norman, his friends, and Orez. But there was no sign of them. They must have decided to play in the tulip tree grove that stood out of sight of our apartment.

1980

TRANSLATED BY MARGARET R. AGUSTA

Mother's Wall

THE SIGHT OF MY MOTHER and her twin left me completely stunned and I stepped back, a table's length away, from the two women. Dear God, there were two identical figures seated before me. Mother, a woman I admired for her ability to accept her children's criticisms, was today seated face to face with her double. It was astounding. Her twin's slender figure, the shape of her body, her clothes, jewelry, head, hairstyle, neck, arms, fingers, feet, shoes, everything... every little thing was exactly the same. Her eyes, nose, cheeks, ears, the sparkling row of white teeth, even her smile and her laugh were one hundred percent the same. And so lively was their discussion that they stood to make a point and, goodness, when standing they were even the same height.

Mother had asked me to be present at this meeting, one that she said would be the most important in her life. She had chosen a room in an expensive hotel. Father and my younger siblings had not been invited to witness the event, and perhaps just as well. But who was this woman who looked exactly like Mother?

We entered at the very same time that my mother's twin had come in, but through which door she'd entered I didn't know. The specially reserved room had apparently been waiting quite some time to witness this event. The bed, the set of chairs, the flowers in the vase were in a state of silence, as if aware of what was going to happen. Curtains filtered the sunlight entering the room. The coolness of the air conditioning slowed down the meeting's pace. Mother and the woman sat facing each other. I positioned myself near enough to be able to hear their conversation but far enough not to disturb their meeting. Three glasses of orange juice on ice kept us company.

"The time has come for me to cut through the horizon and become human," the woman said.

"That would mean losing my shadow," Mother answered.

"And a good thing too! You're just like every other human, always wanting to be God."

"No. Not everybody wants to be God. I don't. Why even mentioning the very name makes me frightened," Mother responded.

"And for me, too, trying to become human has been very hard. My decades of effort have only just begun to bear fruit. It's fair, isn't it, man becomes God and shadows become mortal?"

"But I would lose my shadow."

"And what would you lose?"

"A lot! More than losing one's husband or lover."

"Would it be all that hard?"

"Much more."

"I don't believe you."

"You don't know what it's like."

"Look at me," the woman cried as she got up from her chair to stand by the light. "I don't have a shadow either."

"But that's because you're already a shadow!" Mother interrupted.

As witness to this scene I was astounded. I had to go to the bathroom. There, I splashed water on my face. In the mirror I saw myself drenched, water running down my shoulders, soaking my shirt and trickling down my chest and back. That woman represented the highest achievement possible for a shadow. Thus, the secret of the woman who sat before Mother was now revealed. I returned to my seat dripping with water. The two women turned to look at me momentarily but then resumed their conversation. Was I to regard them both as my mother?

"Will you still pay your bet?" the woman asked Mother.

"Naturally," Mother answered.

"And you don't have any hard feelings?"

"That's enough, don't pry. Keep in mind that I'm not your shadow to carry out your bidding. What would happen if I were a person who couldn't keep a promise?"

"That would be no problem," the woman replied. "We could go on living, side by side and loving one man, the Father of the young man who is present here."

I frowned listening to their words. I was beginning to feel distinctly uncomfortable. I was allowed to be present but was not allowed to speak. I was just an onlooker. I didn't like being mentioned in a conversation that I felt would have been better left unspoken. Annoyed, I stood up. And for a moment there appeared in the room a series of images: my younger siblings running around happily, my older brothers and sisters now in school abroad scurrying among autumn's fallen leaves, secretaries walking back and forth from one room to another, bodyguards practising riflery and martial arts, foreign and local clients in an orderly queue waiting to see my Mother, relatives from near and far having garden parties and their pictures taken together. And Father, too. Yes, Father did not seem to have changed. Someday in heaven he would most probably be just the same: a pipe in his mouth and pacing the floor aimlessly. And not caring, even for instance if one of his tankers were sunk by a missile in the Gulf War. He was probably the kind of man the company needed, one unmoved by luck or misfortune. The hundreds of billions of rupiah that circulated through our company did not affect Father's behavior.

What kind of pact had Mother made with this woman? What did their words mean? What was the significance of this meeting to which I had been invited? Was this imaginary or was it real? Could I doubt the verity of this event? Was I dreaming?

"Who willed your presence in our world?" Mother's muttering did not sound like a question.

"The fine ambition of my own mind, you know that very well, so stop pretending," the woman said with certainty. "You know very well that a company worth hundreds of billions rupiah is the result of ambition. Now it is my company, too."

"That is not what I meant."

"Whatever you mean, the answer will be the same, even though our positions may differ."

"When I made that bet, I was sure that you would not be able to change places with me. Your world is intangible."

"But the fact is I was able to leap across that very high line to reach you..."

"Not so fast, I haven't finished," Mother retorted. "What I meant about the difference between our worlds is that my situation is characteristically different from yours. I was born from an initiative, whereas you were the result of my own wishes. You come from a world that does not exist."

"If I might add to that explanation, I was born of your own misjudgment. Why did you take me seriously when I suggested the bet?" the woman asked.

"Because I'm a successful businesswoman and my company's success is the result of my seriousness. That's the only answer there is. Your bet was an interesting one which I accepted because of its very improbability" Mother replied.

My chest and back were dry but drops of water still dripped from my hair. The three glasses of orange juice remained untouched in their places. Mother and the woman lit a cigarette. Could I call both of them my Mother?

"I'd like to ask you again, who was it that willed your existence?"

"You yourself," the woman replied.

"Was my will really that great?"

"It really was."

"In making that bet I hoped that you would become human. This means then that God has answered my prayer, though it also means the end of me," Mother continued without hesitation. "It makes me happy to know that God has noticed me."

"Obviously you, the origin of shadow, my source, possess something that made God notice you," said the woman curiously.

"I don't know. Perhaps God fulfilled our wish simply because it was an impossible wish to begin with."

"So God is interested in impossible things?"

"I don't know. Perhaps this is His first creation since He created the world..."

"Well, if that's true, I'm glad..." The woman put her cigarette out in the ashtray. She drank her orange juice and smiled. The satisfaction that radiated from her smile filled the room. I was overwhelmed. Though I was staring at her, I seemed blinded by my mystification and awe, though it might have been my fear as well.

If this meeting meant the end of my Mother's life, then the woman who was originally her shadow would take her place. How awful: Could I ever trust this woman shaped from my mother's shadow?

The anxiety I felt in waiting out this game was rising to its climax, gobbling whatever reserves of my strength still remained.

Mother shook the woman's hand but when she made a movement as if to leave, the woman leaned on Mother's shoulder and whispered: "I beg you... Be my shadow. I beg you..."

"That's not possible. It isn't part of our deal."

"But I'm begging you."

"It seems you have inherited my bad trait of forcing people to your will."

"I'm not forcing you. I'm begging you. How could I live without a shadow?"

"That was our pact, our bet!" Mother's voice was shrill with unmovable strength. "Good-bye. I must disappear now."

I found it difficult to contain myself any longer. I wanted to scream at them, tell them that they were going to cause me a nervous breakdown, that they were a pair of useless women thinking only of themselves. But, of course, I refrained from speaking, for I feared that an interruption might possibly destroy the atmosphere of that room, might make this world I could not understand disappear.

Mother began to move, leaving me behind with that woman. She walked towards the wall. I thought I heard a muffled explosion... Mother entered the wall, gracefully, not the least hesitant, as if entering an ordinary room. But then she turned and looked at me. I leaped towards her. "Mother!" I screamed as my open arms struck the wall. Inside the wall Mother stood as if inside a mirror. I banged on the wall and cried out to her. I screamed, I yelled, I pelted the wall with glasses, vases, mirrors and chairs. The room became a shambles. I rolled on the floor oblivious to the shards of glass and other sharp objects. I threw myself against the wall repeatedly, screaming whatever came into my head.

Finally I knelt before the wall, begging in an unintelligible mumble for to her to return. Mother ignored my plea. "It has been decided," she said calmly. "I must remain here. And you must accept it. This is the outcome of the deal I made. Just accept it."

Mother's words filled me with fear. I turned away from her and slumped backwards against the wall. Was I dreaming? How could I hear her voice so clearly when she was inside the wall? How could she still be visible when she was embedded in concrete? Was I dreaming?

As I suspected no one at home took any notice of the shadow woman, which is how I've come to refer to my mother's twin. Father, my brothers and sisters, not to mention the employees and the bodyguards, have failed completely to see that the woman they respect so much is not Mother and has no shadow. But why, whenever the woman puts her finger to her mouth as a sign for me to say nothing, do I obey her? The shadow woman is beautiful, that is true. And as a carbon copy of Mother she is able to run the company smoothly, without the slightest fault, as perfectly as Mother herself would do.

The tender care the shadow woman showed Father when they went for walks, ate, watched television or went on picnics was amazing in that it differed not in the slightest from Mother.

Given this, were I to say to my siblings that this woman is really not our mother, would any of them possibly believe me? And yet I did possess hard evidence to prove that she was an imposter. Thinking along these lines, I've wondered what would happen if my story about the shadow woman would, instead of revealing her duplicity, be seen as a miracle? All the family, the public, the press would idolize her as the world's greatest magical being. Wouldn't that be a wonderful thing for her?

Because there didn't seem to be anything I could do to reveal the true situation, I remained quiet about it. But it was like sitting on a time bomb. I had to do something. In doing so, I did not want to destroy anyone but that woman. Perhaps I was being unfair. She was present amongst us because she had won the bet. No more, no less. Even so, I still found her presence unfair to us, Mother's children. And especially to myself. I felt that she was torturing me. I hadn't done anything to her. Could my time bomb defeat this miracle? Would I have to do something drastic to overcome it? What if my actions were seen as those of a wicked and spoilt child? How disheartening that would be for me.

Today I invited my younger siblings to see this miracle. I didn't tell them who it was inside the wall. I wanted to see their reaction. Surprised at being led into a hotel, they guessed that the miracle would be a dish of ice cream so large that none would be able to finish it. They laughed loudly at their own joke but insisted that I tell them the truth. They didn't want a surprise. Surprises, they said, were old-fashioned.

When I asked them why something miraculous couldn't be found in a hotel, they replied certainly it could, as long as it were stacks and stacks of pizzas. Coming from a wealthy family, what else could excite more joy than talk about food? Every time a new restaurant opened in the city we, as one, would converge to open our mouths. For the rich, perfection lies in a perfect meal.

After Mother entered the wall I booked the hotel room for life. I missed her. I forever felt the need to talk to her. The younger children's curiosity increased when I took them to the room, which was empty now except for a rug on the floor and a few cushions in front of Mother's wall. The other children sat down and stretched out on the rug, all the while shouting impatiently for ice cream and pizza. Oh, my dear brothers and sisters.

"I've ordered ice cream and pizza. They'll be here in a minute," cried Mother, suddenly appearing in the wall before them. Everyone looked at the wall, shouting a deafening response to Mother's appearance. My hair stood on end.

"Hey, what's up? Since when did you make a video of Mother? Man, I don't think the screen is big enough..." the youngest yelled.

"You look great, Mother," the second youngest shrieked. "How come you didn't take us along? I suppose you're stuck up now that you're a film-star."

"Don't want to share the fun, huh?" another surmised. "How come you're all alone?"

"Because none of you wants to keep me company," Mother retorted playfully. But I noticed a teardrop fall from the corner of her eye.

"How come you're crying, Mother?"

"Because all of you left me here on my own..."

Two of my siblings approached the wall and felt it with their hands.

Another one soon joined them, groping the wall and studying the corners. They were surprised. All that was there was the wall. Where did I hide the video equipment? they asked. This must be the latest model, they concluded, one where the viewers could talk with the person on screen.

Without being aware of it happening, I suddenly felt at peace. Perhaps this was the method that I had searched for so long and which I had so easily found to explain or to not explain every stumbling block.

1987

TRANSLATED BY DESI ANWAR

Matias Akankari

IT WAS A PARACHUTIST who produced Matias Akankari from the jungles of Irian Jaya. In the dead of night he jumped and fell back to earth and had come to rest, dangling from the branches of a tall tree. With great effort on his part he managed to extricate himself. Then he rested. And, upon regaining his strength, he set out on foot to find his companions. Before finding them however, he met up with a young Irian male called Matias Akankari.

Matias had taken ill and the parachutist administered some medicine whose therapeutic effect soon had Matias back on his feet again. But this did nothing to quell the parachutist's dismay when he realized that the young native was wholly incapable of speaking Indonesian. Yet it was this Matias who turned out to be an extremely dependable guide and who guaranteed the parachutist's safe return to Jakarta.

So, to be brief, it was the parachutist who first met Matias and who later brought Matias to Jakarta.

Unlike the other boys from Jakarta who had also done Irian service, the parachutist returned to Jakarta without television, icebox, or the other requisites for luxurious living left behind by the Dutch in their former colony. No, this parachutist brought back to Jakarta, Matias.

Matias, who had been his boon companion through all sorts of trials and tribulations and whose friendship he could not forget.

But keeping Matias proved to be more expensive than maintaining an inanimate luxury item. Three plates of food per sitting, a daily total of nine plates of food, was going down that alimentary canal. The parachutist grew alarmed. As a soldier on soldier's pay, how would he be able to keep up with such a rich diet?

But the parachutist was blessed with a nimble mind. He dressed Matias in expensive haberdashery he had purchased in Irian: wool suit, dress shirt, tie, and pinching shoes of foreign manufacture. Then he and Matias rode off in a borrowed jeep towards the bustling center of the city.

Newly come to town, this being the third day of his sojourn in the capital city, Matias was agog, amazed by the brilliant neon-light show, astonished by the height and number of buildings. What's more, he was dismayed by the forest of human beings. Nobody looked like him. His eyes blinked furiously and his head twisted back and forth, left and right, as he tried to capture all that was the urban marvel scattering in the wake of the swiftly-moving Soviet-made Gaz jeep.

Finally, they arrived and, at the Senen shopping district, the parachutist took Matias to a movie theater. There for the first time in his life, Matias was going to see a film. A new experience; he focused all his powers of concentration on the movie screen. Thus when a certain parachutist casually made his exit, Matias was so engrossed he did not sense the deed.

"I want to see something," the parachutist said to a fellow parachutist who was outside the theater, waiting to see the same film. "I left Matias Akankari in there to watch the movie by himself. I want to see just how a primitive makes out in this city. Who knows? Maybe I can make some money from a book about him!" the man boasted to his peer before jumping into his jeep and zooming off.

The film ended and Matias opened his eyes wide to engage in his surroundings. His heartbeat quickened, yet he did not utter a sound because he could not speak Indonesian. His means of expression was his eyes. They stood out, red against the blackness of his skin, rolling in their sockets as he scanned the jostling mass of bodies for his friend. It was hopeless. He let himself drift with the current of humanity moving out of the theater.

Outside, his heartbeat quickened more: Boom-boom! Boom-boom! Boom-boom! The parachutist, the sole mainstay of his urban existence, who he had encountered in his friendly green jungle, had vanished. And now Matias was by himself, alone, in the middle of a forest of tall lamps, jostling human bodies, a jangling forest full of the commotion made by the whirling wheels of automobiles and pedicabs. His present surroundings could not compare to his own jungle's hospitable tranquility. He drifted along, a lone sojourner.

Suddenly Matias heard the sound of a loudspeaker. Ah, a thing he had seen in West Irian on the occasions of visiting dignitaries from Jakarta. The thing cackled fiercely. A pity though that he could not understand what it was communicating. That he drew closer to this dissonance was simply in response to the memories of a remote jungle village where people similar to himself would have drawn together around this sound-giver in order to listen to their own lovely language. But the people around him now were unlike him, and their language was not his own.

For a view of the speech-giver, he nudged his way slowly into the center of the human crush. He is sure to be a companion to the people who come to Irian, Matias said to himself in his own language. But in his present straits, sound was useless. What he really needed was someone who would lead him to a home. Oh, to go home, to be under a roof, to have a place to sleep and food prepared for him to eat... These were the things only a protector could guarantee.

Implausibly hopeful of such a desirable fate, Matias anticipated a helping hand. And a helping hand did condescend. A soft and friendly creature came to his aid. She spoke to him and an alluring expression on her face made his heart beat joyfully. This invitation, for that it was, was followed by a flip of the pointed hand. A pedicab pulled up, and he and this gentle creature left for yet another unknown part of the city.

Upon entering the sleeping quarters of this feminine creature, Matias was immediately entwined and made one with her small body. Big and strong as he was, he was overwhelmed by her power and could not do otherwise since he was the one in need of a friend or a house, or even better yet a small island giving safe harbor. It was finally his! He rejoiced to pass the night sleeping next to this woman who was so kind to him. He woke early the next day. Food and drink were ready on a bedside table.

After breakfast, he was entwined and overpowered again. But there had to be limits to this sort of human activity which Matias had never experienced before; and once it was reached, another form of play ensued. Sitting face to face with this woman, Matias was treated to a pantomime. His jaw slack, his mouth agape, he watched her go through a set of motions for an inordinate length of time. Only when she thrust a handful of paper at him and jabbed her forefinger at his breast and then stabbed herself in her breast with the same forefinger did he finally grasp her intent.

Matias wagged his hand and shook his head to signify that he was not in possession of such papers. The constricting habiliments he wore were the only things he had. So the woman clutched his jacket and pointed her finger at her breast. Matias understood the significance of this gesture. He took off his jacket and handed it to the woman. Whereupon the soft petite creature turned crude and rude. She pulled him over to the door, shoved him out as hard as she could and slammed the door shut. Apparently it was time for her to rest.

Matias turned his body to the left then to the right. There was nobody that he knew. He had been thrown back into the wilderness that was not friendly like his Irian jungle.

He began to walk, a remarkable thing to do in a city where walking for several hours just to walk would be a feat in itself for people used to getting through life on a set of wheels. But it was nothing for Matias; in his own, friendly, jungle he was used to walks lasting for days.

Matias continued his sojourn, and by the by he found himself at the great church just as evening was approaching. No other path seemed open to him except this one leading to the expurgation of the sin that he had unintentionally committed with that woman the night before. He entered the church to pray for Christ's forgiveness. It was dark when he came out so he sat down on the church steps and reminisced about his village.

Once on another island, so far away from him now, he went to church naked but for his penis-sheath. He belonged to the choir, and the choir would stand before the missionary in a happy jostle and sing. He had joined the choir as a small boy. Few of its members could read or write, but church songs the world over are easy to learn by heart. It was during one of their musical offerings that Matias performed the unpardonable act that had gotten him expelled from the sheath-clad choir. Matias was at the head of the choir and, swept away by the melody of the hymn, he pulled off his penis-sheath and began to wield it as if it were a pendant flute. He had drilled holes in his sheath and now he had a flute! Avidly the congregation listened to this novel form of accompaniment before collapsing in a fit of merriment. The worshipful spirit had been destroyed. Matias was reprimanded by the missionary and inveighed against by the other members of the choir. He was kicked out of the choir... Nevertheless, he liked to keep his penis-sheath with him at all times. Wherever he went so did it. Presently he reached inside his shirt, took it out, and began to blow into it softly, softly, and gently.

Darkness progressed yet Matias could see, in the distance, a bobbing figure coming his way. He observed the growing shape more carefully; it was a young man with a portfolio in hand. As the figure grew closer, Matias discerned the reason behind the man's curious gait; the soles of this person's shoes had come loose, thus compelling the man to lift each leg up high before setting it down before him. Yet hampered as he was, this man had come to church. The man went in. After a while he came back out.

"This church is always open; it's different from the other churches in this city," the young man commented as he sat down next to Matias. Although he was carrying a portfolio, his clothes would have been better consigned to the ragpicker. Matias on the other hand was turned out in the best sort of haberdashery: an imported long-sleeved dress-shirt, a tie, and woolen trousers.

Matias did not understood a word, but the young man did not know this and kept on talking. "I'm so tired. I walked all over the city today and now the soles of my shoes are flapping like lizards' tongues. I have a college degree but I can't find myself a job," he said as he tried to clamp the shifty lizard-tongues shut.

Matias observed him. Then he took off his shoes and proffered them to this unemployed college graduate. "These shoes do torture me," Matias declared in native elocution. "No shoes did I wear in the great jungle, even there, where many thorny and prickly plants grow among the trees. My feet bled not. Yet these shoes do now make my feet bleed. Here, take them away from me!"

To the young man's ears Matias' words were gibberish, but with his eyes he came to understand that a new pair of shoes were being transferred to his feet.

From the church stoop, the two men walked to Banteng Field. Wordlessly they laid themselves down to sleep under the colossal statue there of another young Irian male but who had been caught for posterity's sake in the act of breaking free the shackles on his wrists. They slept soundly.

The college graduate woke early the next morning but was afraid to wake Matias. If he were to do so he would be obliged to keep him by. What a pair they'd make. They would create a sensation wherever they went. So in manner of leave-taking, he slipped a letter into Matias' shirt pocket.

When Matias woke up, his friend was not there. He noticed that he had a piece of paper on his person. He turned the piece of paper this way and that, but could make nothing of it since he was an unlettered man. He crumpled it up and threw it as far away as he could, then returned to his sleep on the cold marble tiles. Gusts of wind crossing Banteng Field feathered and chilled him in his sleep.

When he next woke, Matias found that the day had turned to night. Hunger reigned in his belly, but he could still walk.

He passed into an area full of homeless beggars. In this place he came upon a woman pregnant and lying on a heap of paper refuse. She was about to give birth. He remembered how the Christ-child was born over a pile of straw and was swaddled in rags. Now here was another Christ-child coming into the world but over a pile of refuse! It started to rain as the woman waited phlegmatically for her child to come out. She was fortunate; she had a piece of plastic which she then draped over herself. That was her roof; beneath her was still paper.

Matias peeled off the clothes which were binding him and gave them to this woman who was about to bring forth a child into the world. "Thank you, thank you..." she said to Matias who had returned to his original dress. His penis-sheath was back in place. In this manner he waited on her. The rain, coming down harder and harder, turned into a deluge. But he waited until she came out of labor. Then he could do no more for her. He resumed his walk under the heavy downpour.

And that is how he arrived at the city's greatest thoroughfare, Thamrin Boulevard, barricaded on both sides by tall multi-layered buildings. The boulevard led him nearer and nearer to Hotel Indonesia. His wonderment grew over the host of automobiles that were beginning to collect about him. Even though it was raining these speeding vehicles had to slow down and some of them even stopped for a closer look at him. One of the automobiles contained a dark-colored man, a man like himself, who was wearing a suit and sitting next to a beautiful girl. As the automobile came to a stop its passengers turned to look at him. Matias found himself staring back at a person who was like himself. He sprung onto the rear of the automobile and clung on. The automobile roared forwards but to no avail. Matias had a good grip on it. The automobile rushed into the drive of Hotel Indonesia and stopped under the porte cochere where it disgorged the dark-skinned man. Matias had guessed wrong. The man was not one of his own people. The man was an American negro.

A host of uniformed men appeared. Their bodily motions and circling tactics told Matias that they were intending to capture him. He ran back into the pelting rain. Maybe because they were afraid to get wet, the groups of uniformed men gave up the chase.

Matias had escaped but then he sensed that he was still being pursued. Indeed, a man in a raincoat was now running after him. So like an arrow zinging away from a taut bow, Matias ran faster down the great boulevard until he found himself before one of the great multi-layered buildings. He dashed inside, sighted the small narrow room open to him, and spurted in. The room closed shut, and with him in its maw, began to rise up. Finally it stopped, and when its doors opened, another room slid into view. This room was cavernous but dimly lit except for the far end where there was an illuminated platform and a group of women dancing on it. They wore body-covering exactly the way he did except theirs were not of the prominent sort. They were doing a wonderful new interpretation of the dances of his own village. He relished that. Matias step-hopped to the stage, just as he was, in his penis-sheath, and joined the women in their dance. The sound of applause rose from the shadows.

With that episode, his sojourn drew to a close. The city dailies featured the story of how Matias was recovered by his benefactor, the parachutist. It ended in the only way it possibly could, serendipitously.

In fact, Matias was given a goodly sum of money. With this he was able to secure a return back to his beloved village.

At home they all wanted to hear his story. And he told them that in Jakarta, the "high class" was replicating what they, in Irian, already had. Folks just like to wear penis sheaths.

1975

TRANSLATED BY MARY LOU WANG

The Fence

THE RAIN CAME PELTING DOWN. The old man had come to seek shelter under the eaves of our house. Through the window I saw him hunched over as if bowed by the weight of the cane in his hand.

Mother extinguished the lamp in the room, drew back the curtain, and peered through the window. "Don't let him know we're watching him. Next thing you know he'll be knocking at the door," she whispered to Father and me. She released the curtain to let it cover the window and hide the man.

"We ought to have built a fence," she complained. "They come into our yard just as they please. Goats come in and destroy the plants. Children come in chasing after balls and running about as if they're on a soccer pitch. Their screaming at each other is liable to make you deaf. We ought to have built a fence."

Father put down the book he was reading and looked straight at Mother. "Let them enjoy what we have. Just let them be. What's the good of a fence if there's nothing that needs protecting?"

"Do you think this house doesn't need protecting?"

"Not the house. Who's going to steal the house? It's what's inside a house that needs protecting. That's the function of a house, to protect its contents. So, if there's nothing of value in the house, there's no point in having a fence. And because there's nothing in this house worth protecting, for the time being at least, there's no need for a fence."

"So, you think we aren't worth protecting? You think we're no better than the grounds outside, which anyone can walk all over as they please?"

Father said nothing to this but took his pipe from its pouch and tamped some tobacco into its bowl. The bowl of tobacco slivers caught fire with the touch of his lighter. His cheeks puckered as he inhaled the smoke, then expelled it through his nostrils.

"The sort of fence that you have in mind is not the kind of fence that's needed to protect you," he said. "Anyway, sometimes you have to go out through the fence, which means it will have lost its purpose." He took another few puffs and the smoke rose in swirls above his head. "So what kind of fence is it that's needed for protecting people?" He removed his pipe from his mouth and pointed the stem emphatically at Mother. "It's faith in God and remembering the principles of faith! That's what you have to instill in yourself and the children. That's what's needed to serve as a fence in this life." Father returned the pipe firmly to his mouth and picked up his book again. It was obvious that, as far as he was concerned, the matter was closed.

But Mother still had to have her say. "You always change the subject. Do you know what that man is up to out there? Is it really just shelter he wants? If you don't watch him he'll be spreading a mat out there and making himself right at home. It's going to be a reception center for vagrants out there under the eaves."

I couldn't resist getting up then to take a peek myself. I was just tall enough to look out the window. Sure enough, under the eaves was not just the old man who had come earlier to seek shelter but more than five other people as well. They were all rubbing their chests to keep warm against the cold.

When I told Mother what I'd seen, she started in on a long grumble.

"There, that's the use of a fence for you. Before you know it, there will be ten of them out there. And pretty soon they'll be knocking at the door to ask for pillows."

"If they knock, let them come in," Father said, still absorbed in his book.

And knock they did, hard and repeatedly.

"Open the door," Father said calmly.

"Don't!" Mother insisted.

"Tell them to come in."

"Don't!"

"They're knocking again," I said.

"Tell them to come in!"

"But Mother said not to."

"Open the door!"

I went to the parlor and drew the curtain aside again. Several men were knocking at the door.

"Who is it?" I asked.

"Us," they answered.

"What is it?"

"The old man is freezing to death. He's gone all stiff."

I finally opened the door. "What can we do to help?" I asked, still unwilling to actually let them inside.

"Give him some hot coffee and some balsam ointment or some other kind of medicine."

I turned around and relayed this message to my parents.

"Give him some hot coffee," Father consented.

"But there's only enough coffee and sugar for one cup," Mother said.

"Give it to him anyway." He got up, went to the parlor door, and ordered the old man to be brought inside. I took a rug and spread it on the parlor floor. The men placed the old man on it. Mother came in, carrying a glass of coffee on a saucer. The old man took the glass and

57

poured the coffee into the saucer. He began to slurp it, gulp after gulp, from the saucer's rim. His eyes were wide open as he stared around him.

After he had finished his coffee he cast a glance outside.

"Has it stopped raining?" he asked.

"No," everyone replied in unison.

"Do you have any balsam?" he then asked.

"Yes," Father replied, and glanced at Mother. She went off to fetch it.

She was back in a minute. "Rub some of this into your chest." She handed the ointment to the old man. The others took turns massaging the old man with the balsam until the empty base of the balsam jar gleamed. A little while later the old man seemed to have regained his strength.

"The rain's showing no sign of letting up. I had to run for cover five times today. Lucky for me, not everybody's house has a fence, otherwise I wouldn't have anywhere to go for shelter. This rain's been slowing down my trip."

"Where are you headed?" asked a boy who was among those taking shelter in our home.

"I don't know."

"Do you have a place to live?" another older man among them asked.

"I'm on foot."

"But where are you going?"

"Home."

"Where's home?"

"Travelling is my home."

"How far are you going?"

"Let's say until I reach a fence. But that fence is far away, very far away. And when I'll reach that fence, I don't know. So I just have to keep on going, just keep on going until I reach it."

He rose from where he had been resting and looked about him. "Has it stopped raining?" he asked again.

"It's still drizzling. What's the rush, especially since you're not going any place in particular?"

"But there is a place, so I have to keep on walking. And when night comes I look for shelter."

A little while later the rain subsided. The group of vagrants left, going their separate ways. We closed the parlor door. Father refilled the bowl of his pipe, heaping it as one would fill a hole with rubbish, and set it ablaze.

Mother prepared hot coffee for Father, herself, and me. She set the glasses on the table. "Now we really are out of coffee and sugar," she remarked.

"I guess then there's no need in keeping that stoppered jar any more," Father said.

"Why?"

"Because there's no sugar to keep the ants away from. "You don't need a fence when there's nothing of value to protect."

"But the old man said he was looking for a fence," I said.

"That old man wasn't in the land of the living."

"And Mother? Mother's been hoping for a fence too!"

"Your mother wants to live."

"I don't understand."

"Wait till you're old enough to understand."

"When's that going to be?"

But he didn't intend to answer me. "My tobacco, bring me my tobacco. Where is my tobacco?" Father knocked the bowl of his pipe on the corner of the table to loosen the ash. I brought him a fresh clip of tobacco. He tore open its tinfoil wrapping and crammed a pinch of tobacco into the bowl of his pipe.

"Fences. You're making a fuss about this fence. There's no need for it."

"They come in as they please," Mother grumbled. "Children play ball out there whenever they like. Goats come in and tear up the garden. And there should be a fence around the clothesline."

"There's no need for a stoppered jar when you've run out of sugar," Father said.

"But we're going to buy some more sugar!" Mother groaned.

"You don't have to get rid of the jar just because we've run out of sugar," I added.

Mother was beginning to win her argument. "And you don't have to buy a new jar every time you buy sugar!"

"But you *do* need a jar *before* you buy sugar," I insisted.

Father looked straight at me. He shifted the pipe in his mouth to one side. "Really now? So you have to have a sugar jar before you have sugar?"

"Course you do. Jar first, then the sugar!"

"Are you sure it's not the other way around?"

"No way."

"So in the case of a fence, you have to have the fence before you can own something of value?"

"Of course you do. First the fence, then the valuables!"

"All right, so I guess we need a fence."

WE BUILT THE FENCE with money Mother had put by, a simple one from discarded lumber and bamboo. After that children were no longer found running around in the yard outside our house. When ever a ball fell on our property, they had to ask permission to retrieve it. Mother would go out to open the gate and the children would run inside to find their ball. They treated Mother with respect, and this she conveyed to Father.

Father decided to test the fence's worth himself. He set up a chair and coffee table in the yard and would make sitting there evenings a part of his daily routine. Mother would carry out a glass of coffee for him and place it on the table. Sometimes she would bring out a chair for herself, too, and sit down beside Father to drink coffee or to eat a batch of fried bananas. Then, while Father read his book, Mother would crochet a pillow cover. None of the people passing by ever bothered them. Everything was finally safe and secure behind the fence.

Then, three months after we erected the fence, the rainy season began and one night, inevitably, we forgot to close the gate. Sure enough, people came running in through the opening to seek shelter under the eaves of our house. Among them was that same old man with the cane.

Mother stood beside me at the window and pulled back the curtain. We both peered outside. "Don't let them see us," she whispered. "Next thing you know they'll be knocking at the door." She released the curtain and it swung back into place. "We shouldn't forget to keep that gate locked. Now they'll come in whenever they like," she grumbled.

Father, sitting at the table, knocked the bowl of his pipe against the wood to dislodge a crust of tobacco. He looked at Mother.

"And?"

"And they'll come into the yard just as they please. We shouldn't have forgotten to lock the gate!"

"Let them come in," Father said calmly. "It's raining."

"If that's the way it's going to be, what's the good of a fence? They can still come in."

"That's your fault. Why didn't you lock the gate?"

Suddenly there was a knock at the door. I looked at Father and then at Mother. "There's someone at the door," I said.

"Then open it if someone's out there," Father instructed.

"Don't!" Mother said.

There was another knock, this time much louder.

"Open the door and tell whoever it is to come in," Father told me.

"But Mother said not to."

"Open the door," Father said, knocking the bowl of his pipe against the corner of the table again, a magistrate rapping his gavel. I opened the door.

"Who is it?" A group of five men were standing under the eaves outside the door. The only one I recognized was the old man with the cane.

"It's us."

"Is something wrong?"

Without bothering to answer, the strangers, carrying the old man with them, brusquely pushed their way past me. Once inside the parlor the old man suddenly came to life. Mother screamed in surprise, but one of the men quickly covered her mouth. Father rose from his place at the table where he had been cleaning his pipe. The men pulled out knives.

"If anyone screams, he – or she," he added, glaring at Mother, "is going to get it with this knife. Remember that. Don't try screaming for help. In this rain no one would hear you anyway. And we're used to knifing people who scream. A little twist is enough to do the job. So take a seat." He motioned to his companions. "Tie them up!"

They turned the house upside down. But when they discovered nothing of value, they began to quarrel heatedly among themselves.

"We've broken into the wrong house. This here's a poor man's house! There's nothing worth taking. The stuff in here is an insult to our profession. Bastards!"

One of the men went up to Father and grabbed him by the collar. "So!" he snapped. "A poor man carrying on like a rich man, huh? What did you built that fence for? There's nothing in here to protect. It was that fence of yours that decided for us to rob your house."

"This is humiliating," another of the men said. "Come on, let's get out of here."

The five of them hurried out of the house, kicking the front door open, then shoving it violently aside. They then took their disappointment out on the fence gate, each of them giving it a good kick as he passed.

I scooted the chair I was tied to back against Father so he could untie my knots. Once free, I untied the knots that held Mother and Father to their chairs.

The first thing Father did, of course, was retrieve his pipe, knock the rim of its bowl against the corner of the table and begin to search for his tobacco.

"What did I tell you? There wasn't any need for a fence; there's nothing of value to protect. Those men tried to rob us all on account of that fence."

"Yes, it's become more dangerous since we've put up the fence," Mother sighed. "It was the fence that made them want to rob the house."

"You mean, just because of the fence, they thought we had money?" I asked.

"Right!" Father said.

"Then does that mean we're going to take it down?"

"No sense in worrying about that now." He turned to Mother. "How about making us some coffee?"

"But we've run out of sugar."

"Then what's that stoppered jar still doing on the shelf?" he asked.

"In case we get some sugar later!"

"I think I'm getting a headache," Father groaned. With his eyes closed, he put his hand on his forehead. "Go get my tobacco!"

1983

TRANSLATED BY D.M. ROSKIES

When the Rain Falls

USUALLY IN THE EVENING, or when it was overcast—as it was that particular twilight—none of us were willing to venture outside. We'd rush to finish washing the dinner dishes and to clean the kitchen, even the ash-filled hearth where our dinner had been cooked. We'd quickly check to see that the latch of the small chicken coop, beneath the house in the corner below the kitchen, was securely fastened, and by the side of the house, under the kitchen eaves, we'd place a row of buckets in case rain should fall. We used rain water to wash the dishes and other kitchen tools; the water we daily carried to the house from the spring in the valley was reserved for drinking and cooking. After these chores were finished we'd retire to the center room, but only after first closing the front windows and those in father's room to keep out the cold night drafts. Gathered around the table, my two younger siblings and I would then open our lesson books in preparation for the next school day. Is, my older sister, would sit not too far away, knitting or patching clothes while keeping an eye on us to make sure that we were studying. And then, except for the sound of my father who, in his room, sang lightly in his old voice to ease his weary bones, the house was absolutely still.

BUT ON EVENINGS when the weather was clear we'd leave the window closest to the table wide open. Lifting our heads and looking out towards the road that ran through the rice fields, we could see if Mother were on her way home. Watching the streams of clouds that chased each other up the spine of the northern hills, we might remain hypnotized, until jarred from our trance by Father, who knew the weather much better than we, and his repeated calls to gather in his room.

When it was cold, even if it wasn't raining, Father would not permit us to go outside and play with the other children. While I sat inside my friends would be playing rowdily outside on the church grounds. To take our minds off the games of our friends outside, Father would call us to his side and beckon us to sing songs from our mother's favorite songbook.

With an oil lamp suspended from the wall above our heads we would lounge at Father's feet or on the woven floormats. Is would sing a few of the songs that Mother had taught us and we, the younger children, would follow along in three- or four-part harmony, depending on our capabilities. As Is sang she kept time with her finger, tapping out the beat of the tune on the mat or against the wallpost. With our eyes following the repetitious motion of her finger, we were soon mesmerized. If Is felt tired then it was up to one of us younger kids to choose the next song. We always tried to choose one that would convey that particular evening's mood. When Father praised the beauty of a song it meant that he wanted to hear us sing another. Such contentment we gleaned from those beautiful nights. The cold was soon forgotten. Sometimes we became so absorbed in our singing that we failed to realize Mother was home.

She spoke to us from where she stood watching us, in the doorway: "Oh, my. The sound of you singing is so beautiful."

The sound of her voice would cause us all to jump up and cheerfully flock around her.

But, oh, there were times when the clamor of the other children playing outside outweighed any of Father's prohibitions. They'd be out front, calling my name, oblivious to the cold water that was penetrating their legs or the chilly air that was making their bodies shiver. Such things were no obstruction to games of running and sliding through the mud. Their siren-like voices drew me outside. It was easiest for me to wait until Father was drowsy or had gone to bed. That was when I went out. But even after all my friends had gone home, I would stay outside, afraid of Father's temper. I'd sit on the church steps and wait there until Mother came home.

FATHER OFTEN BECAME ANGRY with us children, sometimes for no apparent reason at all. We were lucky that his sudden fits of temper usually brought Mother around to our side. "Why do you get so mad at the children?" she'd ask in our defense. "They're just kids. They don't understand anything. Be patient," she'd always tell him. "Be patient!" And when Mother started in, Father would stop and, without another word, grab his hoe and stomp off to the rice field, not returning home until he had been called.

MY FEAR OF FATHER at home was surpassed only by my fear of him in school. He was the teacher and all the children were afraid of him. Some tried to befriend me, hoping that would somehow prevent Father from getting angry with them. But regardless of what they thought, friendship with me did nothing to cool Father's temper. He was just a very cantankerous man.

I remember one time in particular: We'd been given some arithmetic problems, a slate full of them as a matter of fact. Even to this day, if there's one subject I dislike, it's mathematics and that day my father assigned an excessive number of problems. As usual, I wasn't able to answer all the questions. I hadn't even finished half of them when many of my classmates were already checking their work. Making

67

matters worse, under the watch of my father's eyes, I had no hope of cribbing the answers either. I tried as hard as I could to solve the problems but nothing, absolutely nothing, came into my mind. So angry and frustrated was I that I suddenly spat on my slate and wiped it clean with my hand. My bench partner immediately started to scream and in a second every face in the room — Father's included — was turned in my direction.

Father jumped from his chair and in less than a moment was standing beside me. I didn't have the nerve to look up but I felt his hand on my head and his fingers slowly take hold of a bunch of my hair. I was yanked straight upwards and pulled off my bench. Kicked down the aisle and out the door, I ran wailing home.

NOT TOO FAR from our place, the segmented rows of rice fields began, stretching outward and climbing upward — block after block — until the foot of the distant peak. To get to a particular field you sometimes had to walk quite a long way, trekking up and down the rolling valley's floor on the way.

Every day, after school ended, Father went out to work in the fields, very often with me at his side. He carried a scoop in his hand and I a kettle of tea. I'd get so jealous of my friends, seeing them playing while I helped Father, but for me to refuse to go along...I didn't have the nerve to do that. Still, I found it difficult to understand why I had to work when my friends didn't and once I asked my father why.

"In order to eat," he answered while stroking my hair. "Yes, you have to work in order to eat."

Then he told me that my older brother had begun to help him in the fields when he was my age and he mentioned how pleased my brother was to learn that I was already big enough to be able to help.

After that day, by the time Father came home from school, I was all set. My work clothes were on. I had a hoe in one hand and a tea kettle in the other.

Sometimes, when we were out in the field, Is and my younger sister Min would come to the field, bringing us a snack. Maybe it was only cassava and chili *sambal* they brought, but hunger made the food change to a delicacy in my mouth. Times like that were such happy times. Especially so because they gave me and Min a chance to play.

With the arrival of the harvest season, school was let out for a week and all of us had to go out to the fields to help Father. Even Mother stayed home, not going to trade in the market.

Early in the morning we'd already be out in the field cutting the stalks of rice, or, if that work was finished, separating the grain from the chaff. We younger ones weren't able to work as hard as Father or Is, but with the wooden beaters we had carried to the field we were able to help, nonetheless. Seated on a mat with two or three sheaves piled in front of us we'd use the arm-sized clubs to beat the stalks until all the kernels had been loosened. Little by little only the chaff remained. It was nice working together like that and Father appreciated our help.

Towards midday Mother would go fetch a pot of cooked rice. And sitting out there in the heat, surrounded by the expanse of fields, the food Mother brought us seemed for some reason to taste extra good.

IN THE DRY SEASON drought threatened the paddy fields as the river could not supply all the fields' needs for water. Farmers had to work very hard to save their crops, especially so if the color of the stalks hadn't yet changed. To not work hard meant giving their crop to the field mice and paddy rats.

I had to accustom myself to the cold as I waited long into the night, and as often as not had to wait until all the other farmers had gone home before our field could fill with water. Sometimes, if everyone else had gone home, I'd close the water gates to the other fields so that all the water flowed into our field. But those times were rare. And anyway, why not? All the others — farmers much older than me — usually gave me no more than a dribble, a pisspot's worth, as if they held ultimate authority over the source of the water in the river's upper reaches. It made you think that we didn't do our share of the work keeping the irrigation system in running order.

I was fairly certain that if the water had been equally divided, into three parts, for example, all of us would have gotten enough. But that's not the way it worked. To make sure that we got our share, I always had to make my way to the water's source and control the flow from there. I knew that if I didn't the water for our section would be diverted and we wouldn't get any at all.

So, even though it was night, and even though the men knew that a boy my age didn't usually have the courage to walk alone through the dark and quiet valley, I had no other choice. It was a godsend if I found someone to go with me. With a friend along, I wasn't afraid to walk through the narrow and brushy path. I no longer heard the hoot of the owl that seemed pursue me when I was alone. But if there was no one to go along, and I was forced to make the walk myself, I could do nothing but try to suppress my fear and anxiousness. During those times, for some reason, I felt much closer to God.

THERE WAS A TIME when Mother seemed to be rarely at home. She'd be gone for several days at a time. But we were used to her absences and even the youngest in the family accepted them as normal. We didn't ask where she had gone or when she would be returning. We stayed home, Father and I tending the field alone.

Even when Mother was at home, early mornings would find her at the side of the road with a roll of gunnybags under her arm. By afternoon, when she returned home, the sacks would be full of the rice she had purchased, little by little, from local people. She was known as a fair trader and people liked to sell their rice to her.

The next day, if it were the day for trading rice, she'd rent an oxcart to transport her sacks to the rice market. From there she'd return home with bundles of clothing and household goods. Then, on general market day, she'd take her assortment of goods to the nearest market (the location of which rotated among villages) but the goods she didn't manage to sell she'd carry home to peddle in our own village. Local people favored the thick, ready-made clothing from the city and were willing customers for Mother. Then, too, she knew local tastes.

How excited we were and how we swarmed around her, whenever Mother came home with a bundle of ready-made clothes. We'd choose the clothes we liked best, try them on and parade around in them for Mother who, meanwhile, would be trying her best not to pay us any attention.

At best we might secure from Mother a future promise for the clothes but if, at a later day, we tried to exact from her the goods, her raised voice would stifle our pleas.

"You don't know how other people have to live!" she told us. "No clothes — just bark cloth. Sometimes no food. They're lucky if they have a bit of cassava!"

What could we say? Running through our minds were images of villagers dressed in bark cloth or clothes so ragged they could hardly be considered clothing at all, beneath which were bodies emaciated from hunger and the suffering of that time. Children came to school wearing almost nothing. Trouser legs were cut off to fashion a pair of shorts.

"It's just lucky that you all still have proper clothes and decent food," Mother continued.

Yes, when Mother started in, we could do nothing but remain quiet, that and silently continue our chores. Her reprimands effectively stopped our begging; we could only wait and hope to receive. But days of giving seemed very few, only twice a year for us children, in fact, on Christmas and New Year.

I REMEMBER ONCE being especially anxious, waiting for Mother to come home. Mother never missed a Saturday at home and two

71

weeks had passed and still she wasn't home. It was evening and the air was humid and dank as we tried to cheer ourselves and assuage our apprehension when Mother suddenly appeared at the door, nothing in her hands. She burst into tears and ran into the bedroom.

Father hadn't even moved from his chair before he called, "What is it, Mother? What's wrong?"

Mother lay face down on the bed, not answering Father's question, and continued to sob.

Father rose from his chair and walked into the bedroom. "Tell me why you're crying," he said uncomprehendingly.

"Japanese!" Mother screamed.

Hearing her voice, we all ran toward the bedroom.

"What about the Japanese?" Father's voice sounded increasingly troubled.

Mother lifted herself slowly from her prone position, attempting to suppress her sobs. "The rice," she cried. "They took all of it! There's not one grain left!"

She then began to cry again. Even so, we were relieved. We thought that she had been tortured.

The Japanese were truly on the rampage at that time. Not a day went by that we didn't hear another torture story. Anyone was a possible victim, even respected elders. One day the chief of such and such a village would be called in by the Japanese. The next day we'd hear that he was "sick," that he had been beaten. Or a clan leader had been thrashed with his own cane, in public yet, as an example for others who had been slow to pay their levy of rice.

That had been worrying us for we, too, had yet to pay. Two hundred and twenty kilograms we were suppose to give! Our entire rice harvest didn't approach that amount. It was lucky that Father was a teacher for, as people said, the Japanese looked kindly on teachers. And it was true that, up until that time, their treatment of us was more lenient than it was towards others.

The entire room was still. Father, too, said nothing. The stillness was an anger that could not be expressed, a silent rage within our chests and which our longing for life forced us to suppress.

But silence must, in time, pass and it was replaced by the sound of Father's breathing, a heavy air heaved upwards from a deep cavity, a wind which in vain tried to lift the pressure from his chest.

In a deep and sombre voice Father called us together. That night we knelt before God, our heads bowed in prayers, as Father read from the Bible.

IT WAS ONE TWILIGHT during the plowing season: Farmers were busy finishing their work for the day. Some were already driving their water buffalo home while others were still in the fields unhitching their draught animals from the plows. The sky was overcast and vaguely visible in the distance were the darkening, ominous, hills.

Such evenings always recall for me that time...

Upon returning home from the field that day, Father, as was his custom, went to lie down in the bedroom. As was our custom the rest of us had gathered in the central room. We had no one to wait for that night; Mother was there amongst us, and was not going out again.

Though we had shut the windows tightly, the cold night air seeped in through the cracks in the walls. The flame of the oil lamp that hung above us, over the center of the table, flickered with the conniving drafts.

Outside, the rain-carrying wind slapped at the thatch. We heard a raindrop and then another and another, each one striking the roof harder than the last.

We could hear Mother singing her favorite song, a religious song she sang with deep feeling and devotion. When she sang that song she seemed to be as one with God, as if, with her eyes closed, she was able to taste the life of that world she so often talked about.

For the rest of us, however, in particular my sister Min and I,

73

Mother's songs stirred fear and apprehension, especially so on quiet nights like that one.

I raised my head and looked at the dark and gloomy wall upon which hung a large picture of Jesus on the cross, almost as large as the window. And next to that one was another picture of Jesus, this one with his dropped head ringed with a crown of thorns from which blood dripped. He was trying to raise his head, hope in his eyes, as if unable to endure any longer the suffering of his mortal body.

Mother often told us stories about the man pictured in those two paintings and all about his kindness towards children, hoping perhaps that the stories would dispel the very real fear that was raised in us by the sight of those paintings. When we were alone we always tried to avoid passing through the central room, especially if we weren't carrying a glowing lantern.

Outside, the rain fell harder. We glimpsed frequent flashes of lighting through the wall boards.

Mother ordered us to move. We closed our lesson books, our homework still unfinished, and scurried into her room. Mother held in her hands an open book, her favorite song book. Beside her, Father leaned against the wall.

Mother leafed through the pages of the songbook and chose a song. We followed along, singing in harmony, our voices blending to form a beautiful choir. Our eyes rested on Mother's hand as she tapped out the beat on the mat.

After that song was finished she chose another song and then we, another song, too. Mother then chose a light canon which cheered us as we followed along. So this went on for several songs. So absorbed we were that we didn't even realize that the rain had begun to ease.

Suddenly Father stood and opened the window. The wind threw remnant sprinkles inside the room. Father closed the window and then hurried out of the room and into another as if in search of something. He returned with an old raincoat. The rest of us silently watched Father's every move.

Mother then spoke: "Where are you going in rain like this?"

"The dikes are going to wash out," Father answered hurriedly, not paying us any mind.

"But it's still raining."

Father didn't reply. He went out the back door, then came back in. From the kitchen came the sound of a scoop banging against something else and then the sound of hurried footsteps going out the door and muffled clomping beside the house.

None of us said anything. The room seemed to be a mortuary.

"Your father won't listen to anyone," Mother grumbled, as if to herself. "He just does as he pleases..."

We were silent.

The book in Mother's hand dropped to the mat.

A shudder of fright wracked my chest as the narrow and slippery path that lead to our field flashed into my mind. To the left and the right were steep embankments, cliffs dropping to desolate ravines. What if Father slipped? Who would be there to help? Who would know? Who would be able to hear him calling from below?

Father couldn't have gone too far yet. I rose quickly and went toward the door but Is grabbed my hand.

"It's raining. You'll get sick."

"It's almost stopped," I snapped at her trying to break free from her grasp.

But she tightened her hold on me with her other hand.

"Father!" I screamed, trying not to cry.

"Let him go," she told me. "Don't worry. He'll be back soon."

Is slowly loosened her hold. I leaned back, against the wall, my thoughts still trailing Father.

Min started to sing again, and was joined by Mother, then by Is. The youngest was asleep on the mat. I, too, finally joined in and my thoughts for Father were lost among the melodies.

Two hours had passed since the six o'clock ringing of the church

75

bells and still Father had not returned home. Mother began to worry. One moment she was at the doorway looking outside, the next moment she was fidgeting in her chair. Once again thoughts of Father returned to make us restless.

"I hope he hasn't fallen into the sluice..." Is remarked pessimistically.

The image of the old footbridge over the sluice flew into my mind. The split palm trunks that formed the bridge were rotted and should have been replaced long ago. Yet this was the bridge everyone passed when going to the fields unless he wanted to take the longer route by way of the village.

Mother, followed by the rest of us, went out front and then down to the road that led to the fields. She questioned anyone coming from that direction, but no one gave her an answer that stilled her unease.

"You go back to the house," she said to Is, and then took my hand and proceeded down the road.

The valley was so dark that we were forced to walk very slowly, our eyes peering at the path ahead of us. Mother took hold of my arm from the back. To the left and right were bushes that covered our view of the deep valley beside us. The sound of water racing by below signalled that the rain had been heavier farther upstream.

After climbing the neck of the hill we came to a flat path that lead through a sloping plain. The cooler air of the higher altitude caused Mother to shiver and to wrap her shawl more tightly around her. She quickened her pace.

Far in front of us the mountain was enveloped in pale mist. Below the peak stretched water-filled fields: a terraced lake whose staggered levels seemed held in place by floating upright poles. Water flowing over the dikes of the higher fields further inundated the fields below. Farmers who hadn't already repaired their dikes were the lucky ones, for most of the newer dikes were in ruins, collapsed by the water rushing from one field to another.

Closer and closer we came to the field of our destination but Father still wasn't visible.

"Father!" I screamed.

The sound of my voice echoed emptily from the foot of the mountain. I climbed a higher dike and screamed again, "Father!" But once again, there was no answer, only the sound of the water cascading from the higher terraces. I scanned the field with mounting apprehension.

"He's not here," I heard Mother mutter as her eyes, too, searched the fields, one after another.

"There's nothing more we can do about your father here," Mother grumbled. The way she moved, she seemed to be testing the earth with her toes.

"Faaaather!" I screamed yet again as I walked along the field's rim. Again I heard only the echo of my own voice in reply. But then, the shape of a man appeared below the dike of the last field, a dim outline behind the falling water. I stopped in my steps.

I felt a rush of hope as I screamed once more. "Father!"

"Heeey!" I heard surprise in Father's voice.

"Father!" I shouted again while jumping into the water. He seemed to have only half a body but then he raised himself and the rest of his body became visible, too.

"I'll be home soon!" he cried. "I just have this last one here to finish!"

No one could know how happy I felt when hearing the sound of his voice. Father was alive!

"Almost all the dikes collapsed," Father screamed while scooping mud with his hands. "This is the only one that didn't."

I watched Mother as she made her way around the field, then I set to helping Father repair the collapsed dike.

1956

TRANSLATED BY JOHN H. MCGLYNN

Paris, June 1988

PARIS, ONE SEARING AFTERNOON... For a half hour now the young woman had stood in front of the closed wooden door, but still she heard no sign of anyone coming to open it. With the summer air baking her each and every pore, she became more and more tempted to kick in the arrogant door. One more time I'll knock and if no one answers, she resolved, I'm going to beat it down.

This time she pounded the wooden door with all her strength and only a few seconds later she heard from behind the door weighted footsteps and a phlegm-clotted cough. The sudden appearance of a white and wrinkled face with thick cruel lips caused her to start. Her own mouth dropped at the sight of a thin string of saliva hanging from the corner of the middle-aged woman's mouth.

"*Bonjour*," the young woman nodded politely.

"What do you want?"

"I got the address of this pension from Monsieur Magnat. Do you still have an empty room?"

"*Quoi?* Are you crazy?" the middle-aged woman snapped, releasing with her hoarse voice a mist of brown saliva that sprayed the young woman's face. "This is June. How do you expect to find a room in the middle of Paris?"

"But Monsieur Magnat..."

"That idiot," she coughed, "there's no room!"

"Not even a storeroom?" the young woman pleaded.

The old woman stared at her with surprise. "If it's just a small room with a mattress but no table, *alors*, there is one. But you have to share the bath. I can give you a discount, but you got to pay one month in advance. Here, in this pension, a tenant has to stay for a minimum of three weeks."

"Fine!" the young woman answered without another thought. Smiling brightly, she picked up her black backpack.

The old woman opened the wooden door wider. "Follow me!"

The two of them traversed a long corridor, its walls filled with graffiti: sketches of male genitalia with drops of red dripping from the tip of each penis. Astonished by the sight, the girl stopped to look in closer detail at one of the sketches.

"That masterpiece, that's Marc's... He's a mad one, yes, but his paintings are amazing. Look at that. It's beautiful, isn't it?" The woman chortled.

The girl frowned. There has to be something wrong with either that woman's sight or with mine, she thought while continuing the trek behind the sluggish steps of the older woman.

"Marc's room is right next to yours. The only difference is that his is bigger and better furnished. He needs space to express his art. Don't be surprised if you hear sweet voices. Marc creates unexpected things, ones that more conventional tongues might find difficult to swallow. But I'm sure you'll get to like him..."

The woman opened the door to a room that was about the size of the bathroom in the young woman's own country. A small and uncovered mattress lay buried under dust and cobwebs in the corner of the room. The girl swallowed. The woman disappeared for a second and came back with a broom and dirty rag. "Sorry I can't help you clean this place up. I'll see about getting a sheet for you later. Oh, and

I'll be at the cash register before dinner, at six o'clock. Remember, you have to pay one month in advance."

THE GIRL STARED at the room and squeezed out the rag she was convinced hadn't been washed for at least three months. She had stooped and scraped for almost four hours in battle against the dust and cobwebs, attempting to clean the walls of their coarse French curses.

Though it was almost 5:30, the sun, unlike in her country, insisted on remaining in the sky. European summers were tiring, for it was not until after nine o'clock at night, when the sun finally consented to lower itself beneath the horizon, that she could begin to relax.

Thereafter, life in Paris became a muted but incessant clamor. Like the atmosphere around Champs-Elyseés: noisy and swarming with people, but cold, everyone concerned with the affairs of his or her own heart, no one knowing one another and no one wanting to know others. The girl found it impossible to comprehend the attraction of Paris, why people the world over came to the city just to plant themselves in front of the Eiffel Tower.

Placing the broom in the corner of the room, the girl took in the sight of the floor. Why is it still gray, she wondered, tired and surprised. Is everything in Paris so depressing? Her train of thought came to a sudden stop, jolted from its track by the shaking of the gray-colored floor. An earthquake? But then, a second later, she heard the yelp of a man, howling like a dog being kicked. The sound of his scream sent a chill down her spine. The floor shook again, causing the straw-tipped broom in the corner and the backpack leaning against the wall to topple forward. The man's howl rang in her ears once more. She placed her ear against the wall of the room. Now she heard the sound of a woman, panting. Momentary whimpers and then more panting. What the devil was happening in the next room? If the man were the Marc that the pension's owner had mentioned, then who was the

81

woman? His wife? His lover? A prostitute? It might very well be the last. The woman sounded exactly like a person being...

My God! The sound of the man's voice had reached her ears again, but this time reminding her of a mouse caught in a trap. A pitiful pain. Yet the man's voice continued, in short gasps, "Go on, go on, don't stop..."

The girl took a deep breath. This place was a mental asylum! And she was going to have to listen to these noises for a whole month? Daunting.

THE GIRL WALKED to the cash register with a half dozen questions and enough cash to pay for her room for one month. The old woman squinted at the thin orange notes that the girl counted into her hands. She clutched the notes greedily.

"There's something I would like to ask."

"For breakfast you'll get a boiled egg and toast. If you want marmalade and chocolate milk, you'll have to give me a few francs. You found the bath? It's in the back. Just follow the corridor until the end and turn left, near the stairs. If the water doesn't come out, shake the pipes. That'll make it work."

"No, it's not that..." the girl cut short the series of guttural sounds she found so jarring. "It's about Marc... Is he alone in the room next to mine?"

"Physically he's alone, but his own world is full of visitors. Heh, heh..." the woman tittered, "I'm sure you'll like him. Lots of women fall in love with him, even visitors to this pension. But Marc is tired of beautiful women. The only kind of intercourse he can perform is with his paint or, sometimes, his poetry in the bathroom. Heh, heh...!"

The girl's throat suddenly felt dry and she tried to swallow. "How much longer will he be staying here?"

"As long as he likes, I suppose. He's paid up for a year."

The girl walked away from the smell of spoiled cabbage. Back at her room she found, to her relief, that the holy war next door had ended. How incredibly tiring, she thought, to howl without direction.

She took her towel and walked the roofless corridor towards the bath. The walls that flanked her now were also chock-full of graffiti, but these were of brighter colors: pink, yellow, azure, and green. Even so, the subject of the sketches was the same: male genitalia. The girl paused and looked at the pictures more closely, trying to comprehend the painter's mind.

"Stop, stop! Don't look so close to the pictures. Stand back, *ma jollie*. There must be distance between your deep dark eyes and Jean Gilles..."

The girl turned towards the sound of the voice. A young man, a very young man, his two hands in his pockets, was walking towards her. The closer he came, the more apparent it became to her that the man was only, at most, five or six years older than she. So this is Marc? No, he really isn't bad looking, the girl thought as she looked at his newly-shaven beard that gave his face a bluish cast. His clear blue eyes set in a weary but nonetheless handsome-looking face stared directly at her. How did he know my eyes are black?

"You must be from Asia. But not Viet Nam... That is why your eyes are black. I guessed from the dark color of your long and sexy hair."

The girl said nothing. The man stood no more than five centimeters in front of her.

"Who is Jean-Gilles?"

The man smiled softly, "Later, later I'll tell you that... For now let me look at your eyes, your black eyes. Janou's eyes are so green. Such a contrast, a contrast! But then, I suspect, your personalities contrast too..."

"You must be dreaming. *Alors*, I'm afraid it's time for me to do something a little more practical, instead – like take a bath... *au revoir*, Monsieur."

"Marc. My name is Marc. What is your name, my Asian girl?"

She disappeared behind the bathroom door.

"Aren't you going to ask me to bathe with you?" Marc yelled from the bathroom doorway.

He received no answer, just the splashing of water on the floor.

THE GIRL AMBLED around the Eiffel Tower, watching the Senegalese and Ivory Coast immigrants forcing tourists to buy real African ivory bracelets and necklaces. While their mien evoked sympathy, their aggressiveness was disturbing. But however irritating these shiny-skinned black Africans were, she was willing to forgive them because of their history of oppression by the venerable *Monsieurs* and *Mademoiselles*. Completely sated with the disgusting whirl of tourists at the Eiffel Tower, she returned to her pension around ten o'clock at night hoping to find the confines of her room free from obtrusive sounds.

THE MURKY LIGHT of the corridor that led to her room seemed to promise calm. But she had given thanks too soon. No sooner had she continued her steps when Marc's screams began to bounce off her eardrums. Someone was tearing out Marc's toenails, she was sure of it! If not, why would he scream so loudly? His cries were certainly not those of someone with a winning lottery ticket. It was physical pain she heard, she was sure of it. There was someone torturing him! She couldn't restrain herself. She had to do something. She pounded on the door to Marc's room. Again and again, she knocked but his screams grew more intense, tearing her eardrums. She beat on the door. She kicked the door.

"Open up!" I'll call the police. Open up!"

The screams stopped instantly. She heard the sound of rustling. Whoever was in there had just released poor Marc.

"Open up!"

There was no sound.

But then, a weak cry, "Don't stop, don't stop...."
The girl shivered.

THE GIRL AND MARC sat together at the breakfast table the following morning. She had to ask him: "Marc, do you think, maybe, I have the right to know what's going on in your room every time it sounds like a holy war in there?"

Marc, the mucus in his eyes offering proof he hadn't bathed, looked at her uncertainly. He mumbled as he stirred his coffee. "*Ma jollie*, it would be best for us to talk about something else. My heart would break if I had to speak frankly with you."

"If you won't tell me what's going on in there, I'm going to call the police. What's going on? Is the mafia or somebody trying to take your paintings? It must be something of the sort. I'm not hung up on mysteries or anything, but whatever's happening in there isn't normal."

"My girl, in Paris nothing is normal. Everything is extraordinary. Now whether that is bad or good, or both... Listen to me. Today, let's go for a walk together. Just the two of us. With no one else, not even my shadow. I'll even take off my body. Let us roam the city of Paris with just our souls. With just our souls..."

The way Marc breathed while he spoke, pulling in rushes of air through his nostrils, made the girl more confused. Was he on drugs or something?

Between hurried sips of coffee he invited her. "Come along... come along..." But in the way he looked at her he seemed to want to immerse himself in the black pools of her own eyes.

SHE HAD ALREADY DECIDED that afternoon would be spent exploring the side streets around the Louvre. A heavy rain seemed to brighten the darkened faces of the Parisians. The girl swore at herself for not having brought an umbrella or raincoat but she had no desire to compete for shelter with a passel of Parisians who forever seemed to look on her brown skin with disgust. In the end, even though splashed by passing cars, she decided to run back to the pension.

When she arrived the pension was in near darkness, emanating a feeling of twilight, though her watch read only twelve noon.

At the pension she found the old proprietress scratching her buttocks and spitting into the gutter that ran down the sides of the pension. Inside the gutter two large black rats were tussling over a clot of phlegm floating on the water in the gutter.

"That's Francois and Francoise. I've taken care of them since they were born. I think they like each other now," the old woman said in a tone of friendliness the girl had never heard before.

The girl nodded and pretended to watch Francois and Francoise with rapt attention. But the smell of rotten cabbage attacked her olfactory sense once more.

Skittering off to her room, she heard faintly the sound that she had come to hate so much. He's mad! In the middle of the day like this!? All she wanted to do was to warm herself beneath the blanket in her room. Why did she have to contend with this drama?

She heard a frightening mix of high-pitched laughter and heart-wrenching screams. Marc wasn't alone. There had to be at least two or three other people. If not, what was all the clamor? Was he being crucified or butchered? Once more the shrill laughter. No, that was not a happy laugh. It was a wounded laugh. The girl suddenly remembered a poem, "A Wound, Haha", a concrete poem by Sutardji Calzoum Bachri: white canvas, rent in the center with a gash of red, and the title of the poem scratched on the canvas. Maybe it was that kind of wound that festered in the heart of a person like Marc. The girl wondered what she should do. The pain-wrenched voice weakened, but was punctuated by Marc's own pleas: "More, more..." The need the girl felt to break down Marc's door also diminished and, finally, she went into her own room.

The following day, Marc succeeded in persuading the Asian girl to go for a walk with him along the brown and dirty Seine. During the walk he spoke of little except his youth in Lyon with his parents and five older brothers. He said that his family was trapped in an intellectual sphere that made it difficult for them to mix with the lower strata of French society. The girl knew then what social class Marc came from. But she saw no relevance between his origins and the screams that pealed in his room every four hours.

"There is only one woman in my life," Marc added. "And her name is Janou. We met when we were at drama school in this miserable city."

The girl paused momentarily. Was it Janou's voice she heard? "And so? I guess I'm not smart enough to see the connection between Janou and your screaming."

"Oh, *ma cherie*, Janou is beautiful.... Green eyes, slender, a perfect body for a model, though she might not be as bright as you. Janou is in my hair, my pores, my heart. She has permeated my soul. She feels a part of me, she wants to own me, but, I don't know why, there's something that she has not yet reached... My paintings. When I paint, Janou disappears, completely disappears. All that is there is an object. An object. Jean-Gills. Jean-Gilles..."

By this time, the girl was completely frustrated. "Who is Jean-Gilles? Tell me who is he?"

"Jean-Gilles?" Marc shrieked at the girl in surprise. "Jean-Gilles? Haven't you ever been to the Modern Art Museum in Paris? My God. There is a painting of mine there entitled Jean-Gilles for which the French government offered tens of thousands of francs. And you don't know who Jean-Gilles is?!" Marc ripped open the zipper of his trousers and pointed inside. "There, that is Jean-Gilles!"

"Marc..." The Asian girl glanced right and left. "Don't be so demonstrative. People will think I'm crazy. Okay, so Jean-Gilles is your genitals."

"Oh, not as literal as that, my dear. Jean-Gilles is passion and love. Your black eyes can also be Jean-Gilles. And your hair, your thighs..."

"Marc!" the girl stopped in her tracks and glanced at the two tourists on the bank of the river who were rubbing their bodies with oil. "What is the connection between Jean-Gilles and Janou?"

"Janou can not reign over Jean-Gilles. She is with me, but she cannot own me. She sleeps with my body but not with my soul."

"What happened when she found this out?"

"She destroyed my paintings. Many of them, valuable ones..."

"Oh, Marc!"

Marc dropped to his haunches. Tears dripped from his eyes.

"It's not that she wants to own you. It's that she wants to control you. But your soul needs freedom and you won't have it made into a bonsai."

Marc looked at her in astonishment. "What is that, a bonsai?"

The girl l laughed. "I mean that she wants to shape your soul but that your soul needs space and freedom."

Marc mused. "When Janou sleeps with me she likes to tie me up and put fire near my body."

The girl stared, her eyes growing wider as she looked at Marc.

"Yes, she spreads oil on my body, then slides her body across mine until I feel that every bone in my body has been broken."

"And that makes you happy?"

Marc stared emptily towards the cheerless Seine. "I don't know what you mean by `happy'. I don't know if, in my life, I have ever had that feeling. It's all nonsense..." Marc's voice trembled. "Have you ever been happy? Don't say `yes'. I won't believe it..." He held the girl firmly with his two hands. "If Janou is happy I find enjoyment from what she is doing to me. I enjoy it. But I don't know if that is happiness..."

The girl felt that she was truly in a foreign country, not only because of the bitter and unfriendly eyes of the Parisians who looked on her, not only because of the hoarse, chastising voice of the old woman at the pension. It was a feeling, an atmosphere weighing on her, that made her feel foreign and alone. And, though she didn't know why, she felt that the man beside her now was exuding this very mood.

They walked on silently. Together, but alone. And the summer sun of Paris, the one and only friendly creature, descended slowly, following the footsteps of the two young people.

That evening, the girl, towel over her shoulder, found Marc squatting beside the gutter. Below him, the two black rats squeaked as they ran back and forth.

"This gutter is too small for them," Marc commented. "This world is too small for the two of them." He lifted up one of the mice lovingly. For no reason other than the look in the rat's eyes, the girl guessed that the rat was Francois.

"He must have freedom. Go..."

Francois ran about, reveling in the breadth of the world Marc had just given him. Back and forth he ran while in the gutter, Francoise cried, its voice a high-pitched squeal.

OVER THE NEXT TWO DAYS, the girl explored the outlying areas of Paris. She decided to see the city's slums, the areas where the black people lived, before she took a week's trip to Lyon. When hungry, she bought a bagette and something to drink. When tired, she sat and sometimes slept on the city's cement benches. One time, a flushed and fat-faced policeman roused her with a shout and a spray of saliva. Fortunately, she had her passport with her. The French police seemed to take pleasure in asking for the passports of dark-skinned tourists. She never saw them bothering the obviously American tourists in shorts with knapsacks on their backs. The policeman sneered when returning her passport and reminded her that she was not to sleep on the park benches. After he left, however, she laid back down and dreamed of the two rats, squealing in the gutter. Francoise and Francois. But, my God. Francois was now free! What news would he have of the new world he now explored?

That night she returned to the pension, her body bent with fatigue.

89

A riot of music greeted her even before she entered. What was happening? She pricked up her ears. A party. With dancing! Even the owner of the pension was twirling about in the arms of a man. But even with the noise, the party had no air of festivity. She went through the pension, keeping her eyes open for sight of Marc. He wasn't there. She entered the hazy corridor that led to her room and to Marc's. Then she heard the sound of Marc's voice. Again and again. She could stand it no longer. If necessary, she would break down his door to find the answer to the mystery Marc had presented her.

"Marc! Marc!"

"No, don't...!" she heard Marc call.

"I am going to beat this door down if you don't stop!"

She heard a woman's groans. This time her patience was at an end. Using all the strength she could muster, she kicked open Marc's door. But the sight inside made her heart jump to her throat. Marc was seated half-naked and alone on a paint-covered canvas. Yes, alone. He stared at her with a look of incomprehension in his eyes. Tears covered his face. His paint-blotched fingers hung limp on the canvas.

"For heaven's sake, Marc, what are you doing!?"

Marc stared at her without answering. Then she heard the sound of the woman's groans again. What in the world...?! The voice that she had been hearing all this time, the mystery for her, came out of a tape recorder on the floor beside Marc.

"Janou... That is Janou's voice," Marc whispered, not looking at the girl.

The girl felt as if someone had, out of the blue, hit her over the head with a hammer. Something hard kept pounding on the back of her head. What was happening? She didn't know and didn't want to know. Was Marc trying to bring Janou to life? Why? Because he had fallen irreversibly in love with the jail that Janou had created?

"Why, Marc?"

Marc bowed, lowering his body to the canvas that was four times larger than his bed. His arms and his fingers, thick with oil paint, moved in rhythm with Janou's moans. He moaned and whispered, "Don't stop, don't stop... This is the fifth Jean-Gilles. More, more..."

The girl glanced towards the edge of the canvas. Beside it, a whip, a candle, and a knife. What those objects were being used for, she had no intention of finding out. She could only think of Marc's hair-raising screams. Slowly she retreated from the room.

Silently counting the money she had already paid the old woman, she went to the gutter that traced the darkened corridor. Francois, the rat that Marc had freed only days before, lay lifeless at the gutter's edge. She stooped and touched its wilted whiskers. Wasn't he in his freedom? she wondered as she traced her finger down the rat's matted fur. From inside the gutter came Francoise' squeak. From the pension's front room came the riotous music and the stench of foul cabbage.

1988

TRANSLATED BY JOHN H. MCGLYNN

The Purification of Sita

NIGHT BROKE ON HER SO SUDDENLY. Flung into the darkness surrounding her, she scanned the scene, wide-eyed, stunned, and anxious. And so night did finally arrive, though hardly, she thought bitterly, with the nobility befitting a warrior. Indeed, the proper way for night to fall is gently, in a feminine sort of way, gradually replacing the twilight which merely mediates between day and night. And because of its gentleness, the creatures of the world would be able to feel the nuances of freshness that the change of day should bring. But because the night vented such fury, she faltered, unsure how to react. For the first few moments she was held captive by the mugginess which had presented itself uninvited. The air felt so close, so uncomfortable, she thought as she tried to suck back into herself the beads of sweat even then beginning to dampen her clothes.

Agitated, she took a deep breath. The power that was evident in the long letter from her fiance seemed to pursue her; the chase left her completely winded. She couldn't imagine how she might react if he were there with her now.

Amidst the unrelenting and restless heat of an unfriendly Peterborough summer, she could hardly interpret the arrival of his letter as a joyous occasion.

Four frozen years, she mused as her mind suddenly filled with the image of knee-deep Canadian snow. For four years she had to steel herself, had to guard her defenses...

Beads of sweat, a continuous flow, moistened her temples and brows. He, her fiance, would be unable to fathom how she had managed to maintain her good health and her sanity through the onslaught of sixteen changes in seasons. He would not understand. He won't believe it! He'll refuse to pull back his blinders when judging me, she thought, stung by paranoia.

Her entire body grappled with the stifling heat. God, it's hot, she thought, as she wrestled with the flames that were about to consume her.

She got herself a glass of cold water. Through one gulp and then another she panned the world outside her window. Even though the sun was still round in the sky, the thought of the darkness that lay ahead made her skin crawl. She seemed oblivious to the screams of the neighbor's children as they played in the water outside. She heard a different sound, a loving but authoritative voice. Then she beheld the image of Vishnu, the Great King, in one of his reincarnations...

"My dear wife... I know you have no reason to doubt my love for you. We have been separated by a vast and raging sea, one so vast that a legion of faithful soldiers was needed to build a bridge to reunite us... But you know, my darling, even without that bridge, the fact remains that you have spent time in this evil, foreign kingdom..."

The Great King loved his wife... However, after she had been abducted by the ten-headed giant, he spoke no more of his undying devotion to her. Instead, he questioned her as to what had taken place during the long period she was held captive in that alien land. And as his concern about her fidelity grew, her obstinacy in answering his questions perturbed him all the more.

It was so hot. The woman sighed irritably, replaying in her mind the scene that only moments before had chilled her to the marrow.

They were husband and wife, yet they still did not trust each other!

She ran to the shower and frantically turned the cold water tap on full blast. And there she stood, eyes closed, completely motionless, beneath a flood of water pouring over her body. She emerged from the bathroom a few minutes later, her sopping clothes clinging to her body.

Looking out the window she smiled at the sight of the neighbor's children playing naked in the water. Their stark white flesh glistened in the sunlight. Yelling and screaming, they took turns splashing each other until their mother shouted for them to stop. What? She was surprised. It was not yet dark after all...

"WILL YOU SLEEP WITH ME?" A slight tremble heightened the intimacy of the man's voice.

Strangely enough, contrary to the way one might have presumed she would react, the man's overture left her indifferent. She walked to the door, opened it and stood there smiling disparagingly.

"Are you asking me to leave?"

"Well, there's nothing more to be said," she replied calmly.

"So this is what they mean when they rave about the chastity of Asian women?"

The woman shook her head. "I like you, really, I do. But I'm not going to sleep with you."

"Why?"

"Why? Because I'm not going to sleep with a man who is not my husband... How many times do I have to tell you that?"

"Even though we love each other? Even though we've been seeing each other for nearly two years?"

The woman opened the door wider. The man just stood there, miserable, shaking his head.

"Goodnight," she said, kissing his cheek.

GOD, SHE MOANED as she leaned against the door. It was so incredibly muggy! And those insidious flames keep coming back to torture me, she wailed to herself. She pictured the giant approaching the beautiful goddess. Was he, the ten-headed beast, really so evil? Was he, the creature portrayed in the ancient Hindu epic, really so horrible? In what manner had he approached the goddess whom he abducted? Had he been aggressive or had he been gentle? If he really was as cruel as all that, would it not have been a simple matter for him to subdue the goddess? Yet, in the end, she had proved her purity, had she not?

The woman was seized by paranoia. Although her lover, if that is what he could be called, had never so much as laid a finger on her, she still felt that she had entered the realm of the ten-headed giant. God, she thought, suppose that out of the blue my fiance were to show up at my door and find me with him. What would happen? She let her imagination run wild... Her fiancé would kill him; that's the first thing he'd do. And after that, assuming the worst of her, he would launch into a series of accusations... Just like the reincarnation of the Great King Vishnu, he too would scatter pearls of wisdom about undying love and affection. Comparing love to the endless sea, the open sky and so on and so forth, and so forth and so on. But then, like a saint from some hallowed land – her fiancé did, in fact, have a strong religious background – he would say to her: "Even so, my love, given my position and my prestige as a man held in esteem by the religious community, it is only natural that I ask you about your faithfulness, your purity and your self-restraint. In the permissive West, where physical relations are as easy to come by as cabbage at the market, it is not without justification that I ask you about the four years that we have been apart..."

The words would roll from his tongue as swiftly as water courses through a broken dam. And his accusations, thinly veiled as innocent questions, would flow with equal speed, drowning her in her inability to maintain her defense. Her defense? Must she prepare some kind of testimony? Or submit proof that, even though she and the Canadian man had become close friends, he had never touched so much as a hair on her head? Wouldn't the truth of their relationship provide its own defense? But would her fiancé be perceptive enough to sense the truth and to realize her commitment to him? ...But even the Great King Vishnu had demanded that his wife immolate herself in the sea of fire to prove that the ten-headed monster had never touched her.

She felt herself consumed by the flames. The clock struck three times. The other occupants of the building must have melted into oblivion. The morning was so quiet and still. She could take it no longer and ran into the bathroom once again to let the flood of water pour over her. Fully clothed, she drenched her entire body till her clothes clung to her. Behind her eyelids, the image of her fiancé alternated with that of the Great King. "Darling, for the sake of the community, for the sake of my reputation as a man, for the sake of...."

"PARDON ME, but were you the one taking the shower last night?" the old woman whose flat shared a wall with her bathroom inquired.

The younger woman nodded slowly. "I was hot. I'm sorry. I hope I didn't disturb you..."

"Oh, no, not at all. I was just wondering... Um, what's happening with your fiancé? Isn't he planning to visit?"

The young woman steadied herself against the hallway wall and drew in a deep breath.

"You look pale, dear," the old woman ventured, "Are you all right?"

She shook her head vigorously, "I'm fine, really. He's supposed to arrive this evening. I guess I'm just excited, that's all..." she said, hastily slipping behind the door.

Outside the door, the old woman chuckled and shook her head. "Young ladies always get so nervous when their prince is about to come..."

And indeed, inside her room, the young woman was anxious. Darkness crashed down on her once more, leaving her utterly bewildered. Night had fallen impulsively and arbitrarily overthrew her day. "I can't take another minute of this heat!" she screamed as she ran towards the bathroom and the refuge of the rushing water.

She stood there for hours, and hours...

"YOU LOOK SO PALE and worn out," her fiancé observed, embracing her tightly. "Didn't you sleep last night?"

The woman shook her head weakly. "I just feel so hot..."

"But your body feels cold. And look at your fingers – they're all wrinkled! Do you have a fever?"

She shook her head and quickly changed the subject. "Would you like some tea or coffee?"

"That can wait. Let's sit down. I want to feast my eyes on you..." Her fiancé's eyes studied her from head to toe. "I guess we have a lot of gaps to fill in for these last four years," he added, gently taking her two hands in his.

Her hands suddenly felt frozen. So, she thought bleakly, the trial is about to commence.

"Four years away from each other probably isn't the most ideal way for future newlyweds to live," he began. "We've both had obstacles to deal with, I'm sure, like hills and valleys on a road. But the important thing is to ascertain how low the valleys were and how high the hills have been..."

A sweet and diplomatic beginning, the woman thought to herself as she fixed her gaze on her fiancé's face, which seemed ever so much to resemble that of the reincarnation of the Great King Vishnu.

"We both have had ample occasion to run into – and to search for ways around – hazards along the way. Now we have to fill in and smooth over some of the potholes. We have to deal with the realities of the last four years, head-on and honestly... What's wrong? Aren't you going to say anything?"

"Well I don't know about the hills and valleys that I've had to pass, but..."

"Don't say it, please. I know, you're too good for me. I know that you are pure. It's me... I'm the one who can't match your loyalty..." Her fiancé paused. His eyes were glassy as he caressed her cheek. "What I mean is that we have to deal with the barriers that have come between us by expressing ourselves honestly..."

The woman frowned.

"I'm sure you had no problem in conquering all the hills and valleys during our time apart. But you are a woman and women seem to be more capable of exercising self-control. In a typhoon a woman somehow manages to stay dry. Even after climbing the highest mountain, a woman somehow manages to remain strong."

The woman sat, spellbound.

"But I'm a man... and you know what they say: that the die have been cast and men are damned to be less adept than women in coping with the hills, which are not really so high, and those valleys, which are not really as low as they seem. When it comes to dealing with temptations of the flesh, men for some reason don't seem willing to be rational or to keep a level head. We've been spoiled by what is accepted as the man's prerogative. Society grants us complete freedom to give free rein to our desires, without need of having to feel treachery or shame. Maybe I'm a fool but I'm one of those rare men who do feel deceitful and contemptible. I feel so small knowing that you have remained true. I don't know what came over me when I was away from you these last four years. I'll never be able to forgive myself..."

The woman focused on the movement of her fiancé's lips. Yet in his eyes lurked the image of King Vishnu beside Queen Sita as she prepared to purify herself in the sea of flames. She suddenly remembered that the Queen had never been given the opportunity to question her husband. Supposing that she had asked, "During the time that we were separated, my husband, were you tempted to involve yourself with another woman...?" But, no, that sort of question was not raised. And never would be allowed to be raised. How strange...

And now the evening, stooped low, crawled slowly and politely forward.

1988

TRANSLATED BY CLAIRE SIVERSON

NH. DINI

Broken Wings

SHE WAS NEVER STILL – forever twisting her head to the right or left while peering out of the corners of her eyes, or suddenly nodding her head vigorously up and down, and always smiling, a gentle smile that was so utterly defenseless people wondered if she were sane.

She was the child of a *dalang*, a puppeteer, who lived on the outskirts of the village. Their house was surrounded by a growth of plants and was full of *wayang*-style paintings and a set of shadow puppets themselves, the life's breath of Javanese culture. At the time she was born there had even been a full *gamelan* orchestra in the house.

Her birth had been a joyous one, for her father had long yearned for a daughter. He had prayed to the *wayang* gods and, as if from inside their box they had heard his request, they granted him his wish. A daughter was born: a sister for their much older and only son. And she, this girl child, her father's desire, was given the name Prita. It was a good name, one full of hope and promise. Prita was the name of the mother of the Pandawas, heroes of the shadow plays, and by giving their daughter this name, Prita's parent's expressed the hope that she would find as good a fortune as her namesake.

Apparently though, the girl was not strong enough to bear the weight of such a name, or so said the people of the village, because at the age of sixteen she succumbed to a serious illness. Her brain and her nerves were ravaged by malarial fever. The *wayang* gods were angry at the girl for bearing such a noble and honored name, so said the whispers which blew through the village. But Prita was to remain Prita; her father did not wish to change her name.

Though at the time of her illness she was only in the second year of junior highschool, Prita had to be withdrawn from school. It was too difficult for her to keep up with her studies; her mental faculties had been sorely affected by the disease. Since that time all Prita ever did was play with her father's puppets, stand outside the front door of the house with a smile on her face, or keep the cigarette vendor company at his small kiosk nearby.

"Hey!" she'd sometimes shout at people passing by on their bicycles. A smile would light up her entire face but when the people looked around and saw her standing there, they would quickly avert their eyes and speed away. So innocent did she look, it was not in their hearts to tease her.

At home, Prita was never idle. She played with her father's puppets and memorized the plays, especially ones from the epic Ramayana. Those were her favorites for she felt a strong attachment to the character Jatayu, king of the *garudas*. Jatayu, the eagle-like bird who was felled in battle by the monster Rahwana, nonetheless lived long enough to tell his lord, Rama, where Sita had been taken. Oh, to be an eagle! How she longed for freedom, to be able to fly up high into the sky. Ever since she was a little girl she had longed to be a pilot but now, because she couldn't go to school, she would never get the chance to sit behind the rudder of a plane. When she was still in school, before she had been taken out, she would sometimes suddenly sit straight up on her bench and pretend that she was an airplane. With her arms thrust outwards from her sides, she would emit a low, droning sound.

The classroom would fall silent as all eyes turned towards her. Pity but also nervousness shone in her classmate's eyes as they looked on this child whom the gods had cursed at birth.

One day, after hearing that her father intended to sell his shadow puppet collection, Prita stationed herself atop the puppet box. Though she maintained a steadfast watch, the needs of life that haunt people are not easily outrun by feeble minds. Her father needed the money to pay off the mortgage on their home that he had taken out a year before to pay for the one-thousandth day ceremonies held in commemoration of his son's death. Prita's brother had died almost four years prior to this time and, as determined by tradition, when the thousandth-day anniversary came round, it had been necessary to hold a ritual meal...

"Daddy's bad," Prita said to her mother, her face clouded in gloom.

"But Daddy needs the money. When he has enough saved, he'll buy another set, one that's even nicer than this one. You'll see."

Prita's mother spoke consolingly but her father, though still strong enough to perform the lengthy shadow plays, could not muster the strength to look into Prita's eyes. Prita was his only daughter and now the family's only child.

"But I won't have a *garuda* that can fly me anymore," she implored, trying to protect Jatayu.

Prita's mother looked at her husband.

"Everyone here is mean to me. I can't go to school. I can't go far away from the house. And now my *garuda* is being taken away..."

"But Daddy will buy you something else..."

"What?!"

"A cockatoo."

It can't fly like a *"garuda!"*

"But it can talk to you..."

Prita looked defiantly at her father.

"It would be like having a friend," her mother added, trying again to appease her daughter.

"I don't want it for a friend. I want a *garuda* that can fly!"

Prita screamed and ran crying to the chest in which the puppets were stored. She threw open the lid and yanked the puppets from their chest, throwing them across the floor, one after the other, until she found the one she was searching for. In her fury neither god nor warrior had any value for her.

In the end, while the other puppets changed hands, Jatayu was placed in Prita's bedroom, hung on the wall above the headboard of her bed where Prita was able to watch him. The new owner of the set was disappointed to find one of the key puppets missing, but Prita's father could do nothing, such was his love, and pity, for his daughter.

At times the solitude and isolation of Prita's life seem to overwhelm her and as she grew older, she, like most other people – like normal people – felt the need of a friend. She vaguely remembered her brother, long dead and buried, but didn't even know where he was buried. All she remembered, in more lucid moments, was him one day saying good-bye to her father and mother before setting out to go fishing. He was dressed in a tee-shirt and shorts with a broad hat on his head, and he carried a fishing pole and a basket to put his catch in. He kissed her on both cheeks before he left. She remembered that very clearly and longed to feel that same sensation again. At first she longed for her brother but then she began to smile at any young man who happen to pass by the house. She offered them smiles sweeter and kinder than any she ever gave to her parents.

There was one young man, a customer of the cigarette vendor, who seemed to take special notice of her and Prita soon became accustomed to his glances. She secretly waited just for him to pass by the house.

One evening, Prita left the house dressed in green Peddle-pushers, her hips swaying as she walked toward the cigarette vendor's stand. Arriving at the stall, she snapped loudly at a customer standing there with his back turned toward her. The customer immediately turned around and Prita was startled to see that the person was the same young man with whom she often shared passing glances. Prita smiled and turned, intending to walk to the bridge nearby.

"You look very pretty wearing that yellow ribbon," the young man said to Prita in an ordinary voice.

Prita stared at him as her hands played with the ribbon that kept her short wavy hair in place.

"Doesn't your father mind you wearing pants like that?"

The cigarette seller answered, "Oh, she's always wearing them. Her father's gotten used to it by now."

Prita sat down on a bench beside the stall and swung her legs slowly back and forth.

The young man moved towards her, and asked her in a soft voice. "Do you like flowers?"

Prita shut her eyes and nodded.

"I have lots of flowers at my house. Would you like some?"

Prita nodded once more.

"But you'll have to come and get them by yourself..."

The young man stood in hopeful silence but Prita did not ask him where he lived. She spoke only with her smiles.

"Would you like to come to my house and get some?"

Prita looked at him.

"Would you...?"

She continued to stare.

"Well, say something! I don't know what you want if you're going to just sit there, not saying anything."

Prita smiled again.

The young man muttered as if to himself, "So it's only a smile you got for an answer..."

As if having heard him, Prita smiled at him again.

From that evening on Prita and the young man became close friends. Prita often visited his house, far inside the village, and he often came to Prita's house to invite her out for a stroll or for a bicycle ride outside the village. Prita was no longer confined only to her home and the village, an area she hadn't left since the time she left school. She came to know more than just her father, her mother, and the cigarette vendor. She saw strange-shaped cars and trains but knew only what they looked like because she had never ridden in one. And as new sights and new objects became familiar to her, the strange glow in her eyes grew dimmer and she did not stare so fixedly at people who were new to her. Even so, her mental instability remained and her mind would sometimes blur, loosening her hold on awareness.

One afternoon while Prita and the young man were out walking, a sudden downpour forced them to find shelter in the doorway of a church. Prita, protected from the sheets of rain and gusts of wind, stared outward towards the road, her powers of concentration completely absorbed by the combat of the rain and wind and their constant grappling atop the muddy road. The leaves on the nearby trees looked so beautiful and the branches – bending low, then whipped upwards by the force of the wind and rain – reminded her of trails of smoke caught by an upward draft. Raindrops, carried into the church doorway by the wind, splashed against her face. Such a cool and fresh sensation they made on Prita's skin. A smile played on her lips as rain drops trickled and slid down her cheeks. Her features showed no sign of nervousness or apprehension, a striking contrast to the miens of the other people who had sought shelter inside the church doorway and who watched the falling rain with apparent restlessness. The play of the wind and the water that blurred the road and their vision was for them a waste of time; there was no beauty in the scene for them.

Prita suddenly whispered, "I want to fly."

The young man turned to her.

"I want to be a leaf, to move with the wind and the rain, like a dancer..."

"I thought you wanted to be a *garuda*," the young man said to her.

Prita merely smiled in answer.

He then continued: "I've just finished writing about a stormy afternoon such as this but in my story, the people were all afraid. Does this make you feel afraid – the wind and the rain?"

"No, I'm not afraid." Prita shook her head slowly. "I like it like this. I'd like all afternoons to be like this. Isn't the road beautiful?"

Prita pointed in the direction of the road, now a silvery white. Cars passed by, their shapes distorted by the rain.

That night Prita dreamt of flying, serenely, beautifully.

SOME TIME LATER an acquaintance of Prita's father began to visit the house. His moustache and long beard gave him a cruel look, but Prita's attention was drawn not to the man or his notable appearance but the vehicle which always brought him to the house. It was green and like – or almost like – a car, but at the same time a little bit like the tricycle she had owned when she was a little girl. It was a scooter, she was told. Oh, how beautiful its sound was to her ears! She was suddenly taken by a desire she could not repress. She had to ride the scooter. Once, when she was still in school, she had ridden a bicycle and now, whenever the bearded man came to visit, she watched carefully when he left to see how he operated the machine. But when would she get a chance to ride?

When the man was engaged in conversation with her father on the veranda, Prita tiptoed to the scooter. Her eyes filled with longing as her hand stroked the remarkable machine. She had but one desire. She no longer cared about Jatayu, hanging in her bedroom, or about the young man who was probably busy reading or writing at his home. All of her time was now spent dreaming of one unswerving fancy: She wanted to fly. She knew that if she could ride the scooter she would be able to fly. Even the sound of the machine was like the drone of an airplane to her ear.

Twilight. Throughout the morning, the afternoon, and now early evening, a drizzle of rain had fallen. The gentle glow of Prita's eyes had turned to a feverish gleam as she stared at the machine parked in front of the house. She went outside. Slowly and surely her hands took hold of the scooter's handles. She held tightly, unwilling to let go. And as if something moved inside her, she turned the scooter around and pushed it a distance from the house. Then, with deftness and determination, her hands began to work the controls, trying to bring the machine to life.

Her father and his guest were chatting on the back porch. With the rain continuing to fall, Prita should have been inside, playing in her room.

Prita was now on the scooter and moving away from the house and on to the road that lead out of the village. Her eyes were trained steadily forward. She gave no notice to anyone, did not even turn towards passersby. She clutched the handle bars tightly. Her slacks and white blouse, already blotched by the rain, grew even wetter. Her hair, usually unkempt anyway, now streamed behind her and was whisked upward by the current of air that ran up her back. She felt calm but then, at an intersection, turned to the left onto a road that ran up one of the hills of the city. Upward, she continued upward, while imprinted on her face was a look of victorious determination. She felt that she was flying. Yes, she really was flying, coursing through wind and clouds. The persistent dream, the dream that had been with her from the time she was a young girl up to this moment, at her eighteen years of age, had come true. She was a pilot at the plane's rudder, and she carried herself as such. She sat erect, upright, with a sense of earnestness and responsibility. Upward, still upward she went. The drizzling rain continued to fall and the deserted road reaffirmed for Prita that she was in fact flying. Above the wind and above the clouds, she was fast losing consciousness.

"I'm flying! I'm flying! I'm above the clouds! I'm above the wind!" Her screams alternated with the falling sheets of rain. The houses and the shops in the city below grew smaller. She could hold back the rising pressure no longer. Her fingers loosened their grip, then let go. For a moment she remained erect, with her arms stretched out to the right and left like wings. But then a sudden gust of wind struck her on her left side and she began to lose her balance. Angling to the right, a moment later she was falling down. Down she tumbled with the moan of the marvelous machine rumbling in the twilight rain.

"No, I don't want to fall! I want to fly!" she was able to scream as awareness set in, before the final moment. Sky, houses, the hilltop around her...all were tumbling, upside down. Down and around with the scooter. And there was no one there to hear her screams. The rolling continued. Down and down, down to where the slope of the hill began to rise again. There Prita was still. Her head drooping. Red and black. Blood and hair. She was silent, stiff and still under the drizzling rain and the darkness of dusk showering down upon her. Silence swallowed whatever determination had been alive in Prita only a moment before, when she was flying with her hands stretched open wide.

But Prita had fallen and every member of her body was now broken and shattered. Her dreams and her desires to fly had been bartered for a few minutes on top of the scooter whose roar sounded like a plane or like a *garuda* soaring upward and into the sky.

In Prita's bedroom Jatayu clung to the wall above her bed, waiting to be played with again. But Prita did not rise. She died as the bird, her childhood companion, had died. And the sheets of rain came falling down, through the night and into the next morning.

1956

TRANSLATED BY JOHN H. MCGLYNN

Warsiah

WARSIAH WAS ALL DRESSED UP. That evening she donned her newest batik wrap and long blouse, a *kain* and *kebaya* set which she had bought for the Idul Fitri holidays the year before. The batik was not hand-painted – that would have been far too expensive for her thin pockets – but rather a print of Solonese design which her brother-in-law, a traveling salesman, had chosen for her somewhere on the road. It was a subtle Danaris design with scattered floral patterns. These days cloth that used classic or semi-classic motifs showed much greater variance than ever before. There was also a much greater variety of color combinations to choose from. Warsiah loved her *kain*. Danaris seemed forever able to create attractive designs without overly emphasizing the basic motif. The bright brown color was very much in keeping with the mood she hoped to create. Her *kebaya* blouse was a dark green that offset the more somber tone of her other clothing. She also wore a simple, thin red shoulder sash.

That evening she was to attend a meeting at the high school on the west side of the city in order to get acquainted with the other teachers. According to the invitation, it was to be an informal gathering and therefore, for Warsiah, a good opportunity to get acquainted with her new colleagues. She was embarrassed to admit, even to herself, however, that the invitation raised another hope that she forever struggled to hide. Whenever that particular hope crept into her consciousness, she tried to occupy herself with something to divert her attention. Nonetheless, there were times when, struggling against the thought, she wondered why she felt there was anything to hide. What in fact was there to feel embarrassed about? When that happened, she'd let her mind wander, imagining not only future events but how she hoped things would happen. As such thoughts were liable to regenerate themselves, it was dangerous for her to give in to them. When awaking from her daydreams, Warsiah always found herself disappointed that her life was just the same as it was before, so vastly different from her dreams. Nonetheless, this did nothing to prevent her from falling into the same kind of fantasies in the days to come.

As the last-born child of a typical family, Warsiah had been lavished a great deal of attention by both relatives and neighbors, even more so because the color of her skin was as fair as the tawny-colored lansat fruit. Even as a girl, her skin had always been fairer than that of her four other siblings. This had often made her the object of her father's flattery. Whenever her mother ran out of reasons to prohibit the older children from swimming or bathing in the river that skirted their home village, she would exclaim: "Look at Warsiah's skin color! She hardly ever leaves the house, and if she does go out to play she always covers herself. If the rest of you would follow her example, maybe your father would be happier with you, too."

OF THE FIVE CHILDREN, Warsiah was also the pride of the family for having attained a proper education. She was a teacher. With permission from her father, Warsiah had left the village to reside in a dormitory while studying at a teachers' college for three years. In fact the city where she went to school was not all that far away and there was a bus route that connected the two towns. A train offered even cheaper transport, but Warsiah always took the bus when she visited her family for vacations. The bus could stop on the side of the highway near the village. And once off the vehicle, she would frequently run into acquaintances, neighbors, or relatives who could all but hide their deepest admiration for her. Warsiah was one of the few women in her village who had been able to continue her education beyond primary school. In fact, very few young people at all had an education beyond the primary level. Those who did go on to school rarely returned to the village; employment was easier to find in the big city.

After graduation Warsiah was given a three-year teaching contract by the government. In order to save money, her aging father suggested that she, his beloved daughter, find work at home, in the village. Warsiah had originally hoped to see what city life was all about and to get to know another area, but she was not the sort of person to argue against her parents' wishes. She knew quite well that her family was proud of her and wanted to show her off. She was, after all, the first teacher to come from their village after the revolution for independence.

"Warsiah is a real teacher," the Village Head often declared when chatting in the coffee stall where he watched the buses go by on the main road from the capital, a "real teacher" being a teachers' college graduate. Ever since the revolution, villages had had to staff their own schools and were forced to get teachers from wherever they could muster them up.

But now there was a teacher in the family! How proud her parents would be to have their daughter teaching at the village school in the same town her family lived.

Given her youth and slight build, one might have doubted Warsiah's ability to carry out her job. But for her, teaching the lower grades was not particularly taxing because, in general, the level of knowledge was very low. The nation had just emerged from chaos and institutions were not yet functioning in an organized way. The emphasis in primary schools was on making students willing to learn. Warsiah was gifted at doing that, for she loved children and her professional training enabled her to plant the seeds of understanding among her students.

Warsiah's job was made easier still due to her light complexion, which was considered no small attribute. The principal forbade the female teachers to dress stylishly. Makeup, too, was strictly prohibited, associated as it was at that time with a particular group of women, namely, ladies of the night. A woman was allowed to dress up only once, on her wedding day. Only on that day, when seated beside the groom on the wedding chair, could she adorn herself in makeup and jewels.

Whether out of jealousy or spite, some women claimed that Warsiah couldn't be very healthy. After all, her skin wasn't nearly as dark as that of most of the other villagers. "And she always looks so pale," another person added.

Indeed, her face did seem almost colorless, an impression heightened by the faint bluish outline of her lips that was even more pronounced in the cooler times of the year when near-constant rains blanketed the fields. But no matter what one thought of Warsiah's complexion, no one could argue with the luxuriance of her thick black hair which she had inherited from her mother. Her thick lashes and straight eyebrows set off her round, dark-brown eyes. Her nose was small and somewhat flat and her nostrils flared. Her mouth was even and her lips full and sensual. For men this was, no doubt, her most attractive feature.

With these as her provisions, Warsiah began to teach at the village school. Even after taking the job her life went on pretty much as it did before, with no major upheavals. As the village grew new houses sprung up, encroaching upon the agricultural land. As one year replaced another, the borders that had formerly distinguished one village from another blurred until, finally, population growth and a convergence of rooftops transformed the villages into a small city, one with its own parks and even a movie theater. Javanese dance and theater troupes rotated in staging performances in the bamboo pavilion that had been erected in the city square. Time went by, progress marched on, until one day the regional government announced its plan to build near the city a reservoir to supply drinking water to the capital.

News of the reservoir soon reached everyone's ears and became the town's main topic of conversation. The food stall next to the highway where people waited for busses and other transport to pass became the hub of information. People were thrilled to have something new to talk about and delighted when word spread that one of the engineering assistants – a burly, good-looking young man – originally hailed from that same village. Throngs of people gathered to investigate and observe the workers at the construction site.

For quite some time Warsiah's father had found it difficult to allay the anxiety he harbored inside his chest. Three years had passed since his beloved daughter had returned to the village, entrusted by the government to teach the village children to be good citizens. From one year to the next he had remained hopeful that a man would come along who would be suitable in marriage for Warsiah. A male colleague of Warsiah's had sometimes visited but their conversations seemed to revolve around commonplace, everyday matters. His daughter seemed to care for nothing more than discussing school-related problems. The two of them even took the children from the higher grades on a field trip to the Borobudur Temple. Even so, there was no sign that might lead him, Warsiah's father, to believe that the pair intended to pursue a closer relationship. He asked neighbors about their male children, and from a man he often met at the roadside stall he learned about the man's son, who had left the village to study at a technical institute in West Java. In conversations about the distribution of new seeds and other problems concerning their rice crops, he learned that this young man had not returned to the city since his departure for school. Warsiah's father didn't, therefore, foresee the possibility of arranging a marriage between his daughter and the boy who was off at technical school. That is, not until the time when construction began on the reservoir at the city's edge.

Warsiah's father's heart pounded and he felt as if it were he himself who was getting married when he saw the young man who had been absent from the village for years. Delight meshed with anxiety until finally, one day, he found the opportunity to touch on the subject with the young man's father. From conversation after conversation and from jokes to subtle hints, the two fathers came to an agreement to make use of the services of Mak Sum, a middle-aged woman whose skill it was to arrange marriages and, sometimes, illicit affairs. It didn't take long to settle the matter. Warsiah's name alone was assurance enough that she would make a good daughter-in-law. A meeting between the two young people was arranged. They had, as it turned out, once known each other, but it had been years since they had met, face to face, and passing time had molded the characters of these two young people according to influences of their respective environments.

Warsiah was ignorant of her father's intentions, but after meeting the young man, she acknowledged, if only secretly, that he was the most interesting man to come along in quite some time. Perhaps her interest was evoked by the fact that he was always so well-dressed. She wasn't sure, but she was aware of the difference between him and her male colleagues and other male acquaintances. Maybe it had to do with the gentle way he spoke, with his deep, attentive, voice.

After only their second meeting, Warsiah already found herself longing for him. One night they went out together to watch a film at the local movie theater. Another evening they went into the city to see the night market. One day they went along with a group of engineers to visit Ratu Baka Temple where they had lunch. Warsiah was happy.

Warsiah's father finally informed her that her parents and the young man's parents were making arrangements for their wedding. After harvest would be a good time, he told her. Barring plant disease or infestation by rats, the rice crop was expected to be a fairly good one that year.

"This will be the last wedding that I hold," her father said. "The last and the biggest because you are a teacher and your future husband is an engineer!"

Warsiah reflected for a moment upon what she was hearing.

Her father did not try to conceal his pride. Warsiah's wedding was to be the apex of his life until he received God's call. Warsiah gradually came to see that every single event related to her and the young man – their meeting, her birthday party, visits between the two families, and so on – had all been prearranged. Nonetheless, she didn't regret a thing. The seed of admiration that had germinated in her had grown into love and affection. Whenever she was with the young man, she anxiously awaited his embrace. A touch of his hand, a caress of her shoulders... But that never happened. Once in the movie theater, and another time in a pedicab when they were making their way home through a rainstorm, the young man had suddenly turned her head towards him and kissed her deeply. Feeling his long, hot tongue in her mouth had almost caused her to choke and gag. His roughness surprised her but she wasn't bold enough to resist and she let herself be fondled even as she groped for something to hold on to. The same thing had happened another time when they were alone together in her father's resting hut in the rice field. Caught up in the passion of the moment, she was hardly aware that the young man had lifted her dress and begun to explore with his hand the area between her thighs. She had nearly screamed; it felt like an electric current was stinging her sensitive skin. But the sound of her voice was muted, drowned in the depths of her throat, stifled by the man's mouth.

She had never been taught about the origin of life. Even at school her teachers had been silent on the question of carnal relations between men and women. At the dormitory where she lived, however, she and the other young women would share their thoughts, telling each other what they knew or had learned. At a younger age, the first time she experienced a trickle of red flowing from that secret corner of her body, she had run sobbing to her mother. Her mother had gently assured her that this was what happened when girls grew up. Following that her female relatives, one after the other, had teased her affectionately and joked with her about it. They had even held a traditional celebration of thanksgiving in honor of her new maturity. They had given her gifts that day to mark her rite of passage into this new, adult, world.

Like most girls or women, Warsiah daydreamed about the kind of man she would love. She also fantasized how it would be to make love. And in her dreams, the man she loved always treated her gently and with care.

Twice now the young man had kissed and fondled her, and both times reality had been completely different from what Warsiah had imagined. She heard no words of affection or praise. She saw no look in his eye capable of melting her heart. His sudden invitation to make love failed to stir her, for his manner was less like lovemaking and more like an attack. His kisses and touches gave no pleasure. And so, the third time he began to kiss her and to stroke her thighs with his hand, she was stung more by physical instinct than by the softness of the seduction.

IT WAS ALSO HER INSTINCTS which made Warsiah give pause when she heard her father discussing her wedding with the young man. She suddenly realized that she did not know the man very well. They were neighbors. Both had made their parents proud. Warsiah was only a few months older. They had attained comparable levels of education. At a glance it appeared that everything should be fine. They were a perfect couple, a proper match! Still, Warsiah was uncomfortable with the situation and felt that something was out of place. For several days, during the moments when she was alone, she tried to determine what it was that she found so unsettling about their relationship. Her fianceé, as people around the house had begun to call him, was citified. He seemed all too familiar with the ways of life in the big city. Undoubtedly he had, in his time there, gotten to know numerous women. He had probably a thousand times embraced and kissed other women just as he had done with her. The wedding was set for another two or three days. She wanted more time to get to know her fianceé so that she could better fathom her future husband's character. But pressure from all sides held her back. What was she waiting for? Over and over she heard the same question.

Yes, what was she waiting for? She was twenty-four years old and there were many women in the area, ones much younger than herself, who would jump at such an opportunity. The famed temple of Roro Jonggrang which dominated the area's view, seemed to heighten the pressure on parents to marry off their daughters as soon as possible. Girls in the area grew up beneath the legendary curse of the giant Bandung Bondowoso who had foretold that none of their kind would ever marry. The superstition was rooted so firmly in the area that even in these modern times it was hard to escape the curse's influence. Even Warsiah, whose level of education was the highest anyone in her family had ever achieved, could not free herself from the superstition. To herself she acknowledged her own fear of the curse. Maybe this was why she seemed so willing to stop searching for reasons behind her feelings of doubt over marriage to that proper young engineer.

The wedding went off marvelously and the performances that were held in conjunction exhausted both families of their earnings from that year's harvest. They had even pawned future harvests to secure the necessary funds. But for them it didn't matter that they would be in debt for some years to come. The important thing was that the villagers – their friends and neighbors – would not soon forget the glorious celebration. For three days and three nights there had been a constant change of entertainment, from a *keroncong* band to a *gamelan* orchestra, from dances performed by the school children as their contribution to the event, on up to the shadow puppet play that was performed by a well-known puppeteer on the last official night of revelry. A week after their marriage, when the newlyweds moved from the bride's house to the home of the groom's parents, the party began again and continued through the eighth day.

Warsiah was happy and thought that she was truly going to remain happy. On her wedding night and during the nights that followed, she began to learn the intimate secrets that husbands and wives share. With each passing day she became more convinced that she was beginning to understand the nature of the man she had married.

Once a month, for a few days, her husband went to his school to attend classes. He also went into the city for several days at a time to attend meetings with the builders and engineers responsible for the construction of the reservoir. Each time her husband left, Warsiah noticed how long the days felt and how slowly time passed.

Six months went by. The reservoir was near completion. And now that Warsiah's husband was finished with his work he had to return to the city to continue his studies. After due consideration of the matter with the family, it was decided that the newlyweds would live apart. Warsiah would wait for him in the village, at the home of her in-laws. Once a month she would send money to him so that he, still a student, could come home for a visit.

TIME PASSED VERY SLOWLY. For Warsiah, each day meant waiting for a letter or some sort of news from her husband. One month, two months, three months passed. Everything proceeded smoothly, according to plan, but in the fourth month Warsiah miscarried. She had been two months pregnant. From the hospital she went directly home to her parents and afterwards – after the miscarriage – began to feel that something had changed in her relationship with her husband. The doctor had recommended that she rest in order to regain her strength and so Warsiah had gone to her parents; she felt that that would be the best place for her. She was much closer to her mother and to her own relatives than to her in-laws. Her husband came home and for two days stayed at her bedside but then he left again, and a month went by without a visit. Letters arrived telling how busy he was with his exams and the like. Warsiah greeted her husband's news of endless school activities without suspicion and when she was well enough to teach again she gladly embraced the occasion. Back at school she felt that the students were not only more attentive but also more loving. Perhaps that was because during the time she had been ill the class had been taken over by the school principal, known for his strictness.

Semester break arrived and her husband sent word that he would be home for a week, after which he would have to return to school because he had received an important job offer, one that would further his career.

In the week that they were together Warsiah almost forgot their time apart but, in the end she was forced, once again, to realize that her husband had to return to West Java to school. A family meeting resulted in the suggestion that Warsiah consider requesting a transfer to West Java, but strangely enough it was none other than her husband who objected to the suggestion. Such a move would not be good for her career, he said. Besides, she wouldn't be comfortable living outside the area and he himself would have difficulty concentrating on his studies if she were always there, at his side.

A month passed before the Lebaran holiday arrived to mark the end of the fasting month, but her husband did not come home. Months passed without a visit. Letters became few and far between. At one point Warsiah, completely out of patience with her husband, decided to stop writing to him, but her parents quickly intervened.

"Studying at university isn't easy. Be patient! You're the one who

121

has to write to him and let him know how you're doing," they commanded. "Why, he might be sick. It's no fun being so far away from home," they added.

And with that Warsiah's resolve dissolved. Her parents were right. If her husband were ill, he would feel incredibly lonely, she thought. So, in her next letter, she gently suggested that he write. Even a single line of news would do. Better yet, if it were possible, he should come back to the village for a visit.

Five months passed without further word from Warsiah's husband. By this time Warsiah's parents were experiencing a myriad of feelings – from anxiousness to worry, from anger to shame about their son-in-law's behavior. They decided to write to him themselves, and in their letter to him asked if he had received the money they had sent and strongly suggested that he do the proper thing and send them news.

In order to fill up her time, a thing increasingly difficult for her to do without ending up staring into space, Warsiah began to teach evenings as well. Three times a week she went into the city to study English which, since the revolution, had become the most important language in the country after Indonesian.

When all the attempts to convince Warsiah's husband to write proved to be for naught, Warsiah's father-in-law decided to go to West Java and speak to his son in person. As befitting a dutiful daughter-in-law, Warsiah accompanied him to the station. Personally, she expected little to come of her father-in-law's trip. Deep down she felt that something had happened, that their relationship was over, a feeling that confirmed the premonition she had felt from the very beginning. Her woman's intuition spurred her to work harder and to take up a new course of study. She began to appreciate her solitude. At first those long nights alone had been a miserable struggle to get through, but in the last couple months she had come to feel more at ease. Little by little she had begun to recognize that her marriage to that proper young man was a thing of the past. All her waiting for him was distracting her attention and making her ill. She knew that she needed more time to get over it once and for all but also knew that once she could stop the nerve-wracking waiting things would lighten up.

But a woman does not so easily free herself from the past. Wisely Warsiah tucked away whatever subconscious ray of hope she harbored and which would sometimes surface to subsume her other feelings. She herself had no idea what the outcome would be. Would her father-in-law return with his son? Would there be a resolution? Would there be a conclusion, one final and certain word that would prove a point of closure for all her uncertainty?

Ten days later, Warsiah's father-in-law returned. That night he and his wife came to Warsiah's parents' home to see their daughter-in-law. The man had a grave expression on his face. The wrinkles in his forehead seemed deeper. The circles under his eyes formed horrible canyons. Reluctantly, he informed Warsiah that the address they were using for his son was not where he really lived. He had spent several days trying to find his son and, finally, he had found him—married and living with a Sundanese woman with whom he already had a child. As her husband described this turn of events, Warsiah's mother-in-law sat not saying a word. This is just what she herself had feared. Her powers of intuition as a mother and a woman had been proven true. She wept silently, unable to look into Warsiah's eyes.

Warsiah, too, was speechless.

Her father-in-law said that he and his wife felt extremely embarrassed and were ashamed to face Warsiah and the other villagers. They thought that the wedding they had held had been their son's first. In fact it had been his second. He had no proposal for dealing with the fact that his son had two wives.

Warsiah's father and father-in-law conferred with each other. They looked to religious law for a solution. Their wives said nothing. Warsiah was silent, too, as she listened to the conversation. Though she felt a hard and heavy lump in her chest, her eyes remained dry.

Finally Warsiah's father-in-law turned and said to her,"If you are willing to be his second wife, my son — your husband — will come home and stay with you for a few days. It just so happens that school is almost over."

Warsiah did not give a quick reply. Her father turned toward her. Warsiah turned toward her mother momentarily and then said, "We haven't lived together for months, during which time I've completely supported myself. Under religious law, therefore, if I file for divorce, the law will be on my side and that of my family."

"But Warsiah!" her father cried.

"Wait a few days," her father-in-law advised. "I know this isn't a pleasant experience."

Would it be any more pleasant to be a second wife? Warsiah wondered. As tactfully as possibly, she then restated her wishes. Her mother and father added nothing further. But as soon as Warsiah's in-laws had left, her own mother and father tried, in turns, to convince her of the merits of accepting the status of second wife. It would save them from ridicule and mockery. But Warsiah was firm and could not be moved to change her mind. From the very beginning she had known that something was wrong in her relationship with that man. Yet she had learned to love him and had learned to miss him, too. The "perfect match," as everyone had labeled them, had only happened because it had been arranged. They had ended up together simply because the proper circumstances had been consciously created to bring it about. Now if they were to divorce, as appeared imminent, people would insist on finding a reason: she wasn't his real match, after all! A woman usually feels a part of the man who embraces her and sleeps with her. For Warsiah, who had never known any other man, having a husband was the goal of life. Marriage was the epitome of success that she and her family hoped for. And she had found a man, both young and attractive, and also passionate in bed. Warsiah felt a wave of electricity pulse through her body. Her primal instincts had been awakened. Yet, once again, they were suppressed by her sense of self-respect.

WARSIAH DREW BACK the curtain and looked out the window. The pedicab driver who lived nearby was to pick her up to take her to the meeting. She would stop by at a colleague's house on her way. When attending meetings she preferred going with someone else to going alone.

It took several months, working alone, for her to arrange for her divorce. But she had every reason to demand the right to a divorce and the court had granted her request. Once the case was settled, she submitted an application to continue her education at a higher level. By this time the young country's administrative system was better organized and vocational schools had been established in the larger cities and were being run much along the same lines as secondary schools. Warsiah enrolled to study English in the Department of Languages. As in former years, she studied hard and always did well on the exams.

Similarly, as in the past, there was neither a dearth of women friends nor a lack of male admirers far from her side. She began to use her father's name after "Mrs Warsiah." In using this form of address she found some males distancing themselves from her and others trying to get closer, depending on their motives. Some regarded the "Mrs" as a safe sign. Once they learned that she was divorced, however, not a few of them changed their attitude. It was as though the address were a trademark, a symbol of her market value. With a divorced woman, who knows? Maybe she had some kind of defect and it was better not to get too close. The worth of a woman who had been married and divorced was altogether different from that of a woman whose husband had died. Warsiah patiently endured the social backlash that resulted from her actions. Once again she busied herself, pursuing knowledge and befriending the young people she taught.

However she might have appeared, Warsiah did, nonetheless, have normal human feelings and she was sensitive to her friends' opinions of her. As time went on she felt more strongly that something was lacking in her relationships with her peers. She was only twenty-five years old, yet she felt closer to her family, who were all older than her. When it came to going out or attending meetings, Warsiah always took the opportunity to make new friends. Even though old memories would always rise to haunt her, for a few moments at least, she was able to enjoy the pleasure of friendships free from ulterior motives. Men seemed to prefer to get to know women who did not have the term "Mrs" in front of their names. Though the increasing trend was to sport an academic title before one's name, Warsiah chose to include "Mrs" on her diploma and other official documents as well. This title, or her honesty in its usage, perhaps is what seemed to spook the young men.

Each and every time the same thing happened. Each time Warsiah's hope grew thinner. She asked herself if there wasn't a single man in this huge country who thought it normal to invite a woman of his own age to a restaurant or to a film with none other than the most genuine intentions? Warsiah was a woman who, by mistake or by an unfortunate twist of fate – depending on one's point of view – had married and given her body to a man. Even then, that had happened only through the "help" of a man!

But Warsiah continued to hope. For meetings and other kinds of gatherings, she was always dressed neatly and presented herself well. She knew that her femininity was one of her most compelling charms.

Outside the house, the pedicab bell was ringing.

1983

TRANSLATED BY CLAIRE SIVERSON

YUDHI SOERJOATMODJO

Dieng

THE YOUNG MAN in the red T-shirt turned to me: "There's no reason to stay," he said. "The land we inherited grows smaller by the year."

We watched the trucks that plied the roads between Dieng Crater and Wonosobo. They'd been at it since dawn, raising dust. And the children, snot-nosed and wild-haired, whoop-whooped greetings towards the drivers and their occasional passengers.

At the last house I visited, we ate a meal of salted fish and hot sticky rice. Afterwards, our host and men from villages nearby retired to a small dark room with a window overlooking the valley.

One of the men mentioned a "scheme" whereby farmers could borrow money from the local government, providing they switched from growing potatoes to other crops.

In the darkness their eyes were cold steel — *What will happen if we refuse? And if we fail, will they come and take away our land?* — but theirs' was a quiet anger and all we could hear were the resonant cries of children playing war in the valley.

SUBAGIO SASTROWARDOYO

Philosophy and Poetry

SINCE THE EARLY DAYS of writing in Indonesia a close link has existed between philosophy and literature. In the classical literature of Indonesia a pujangga or writer was both poet and philosopher. He was expected to reveal in literary form views of and guidance for life and to provide his readers (or listeners) prophetic truth. *Wedatama*, a Javanese literary classic, and *Syair Perahu*, a well-known poem in Malay, are still revered as philosophy apart from the fact that they are recognized as excellent literature. But it is the philosophy, or *ngelmu* (in Javanese) which put the legitimizing stamp of "literature" on the works.

We find the same attitude in a more recent era in Europe in Martin Heideger, who pointed out the intimate link between philosophy and literature. Heideger says that thinkers, *i.e.*, philosophers, are poets and that the speech of thinking is by nature poetic, because both philosophy and poetry constitute the uttering of truth, the expression of "the unconcealed-ness of beings."

At least in what is known as the *Lebensphilosophie*, philosophy finds the same subject of thought as poetry, that being man (or humanity) and life. As Heideger concluded in his essay "*Wozu Dichter*" the meeting ground of poetry and philosophy is the thinking of man about the basic problems of life which, as formulated by Heidegger, are "sickness, death and love."

The difference between philosophy and literature might be found in the distinct analytical methods and modes of expression of these two fields. In philosophy, the search for an awareness of man and life employs clear and justifiable ways of thought. In addition, the philosopher must convey his views in a written form that is coherent, consistent, and unified. He has a scientific procedure to follow. In literature, however, and especially in poetry, the awareness of man and life is more often found in glimpses of sudden thought, in unplanned discoveries, and in concepts expressed in a "poetic saying of truth." In the field of literature, the validity of poetry rests in the integrity of its form of expression and in the truthful utterance from the "spiritual center." Jacques Maritain describes this as the place where the totality of man resides as the source of creativity. In literature the writer need not adhere to a special method or system in his analysis of thought. He has no need to justify to the reader the objectiveness of his point of view in stating what he feels to be a general truth.

In philosophy, particularly in the philosophy of life, one can find exceptions. Nietzsche, for example, the philosopher viewed by many as the pioneer of this genre of philosophy, made no attempt at all in *Thus Sprach Zarasthustra* to clarify his "method" or "system." Further, the language the author employs in this book is much closer to literary speech than to that of a philosophical treatise. Aphorisms used by Nietzsche and by the Javanese writer Sosrokartono ("rich without wealth, strength without power, attack without friends, victory without suppression"), while absent of scientific methodology, are nonetheless philosophical. So, too, the essays of Kierkegaard, the father of existentialism, leave no impression of scientific thought, expressed as they are in a form similar to that of a kind of church sermon. The philosophy of life and life itself cannot be expressed in a system. As F.H. Heinemann said in his discussion of existential philosophies, "existence cannot be systematized."

WHAT I WOULD LIKE TO DISCUSS here is modern Indonesian poetry and its relationship to philosophy. We can find that link in the basic thoughts about life and man that underline poetry, especially the poetry of authors who have achieved a resolution of total and personal expression. In this instance I will touch on only a few of the poets who have acquired a stable position within the world of Indonesian literature. Limitations of time and space preclude discussion of all the poems by the poets I include in this group.

I begin by stating that many of the poems that are published in newspapers, journals and books today — written by young or would-be poets — fail to express genuine inspiration, the kind that arises spontaneously from honesty of thought, feeling, and understanding. Most of what appears are personal pieces, adolescent literature.

In this paper I will touch only on the works of a select few poets, poets whom I feel have achieved the depth of intuition or maturity of expression in capturing the meaning of human life. These poets are Sutardji Calsoum Bachri, Sapardi Djoko Damono, Linus Suryadi AG, Chairil Anwar, and Sitor Situmorang.

In writing poetry, writers tend to philosophize. This is linked to the nature of poetry, representing as it does an attempt to capture or express something in compact, condensed form.

According to some observers, Herbert Read being one, the German-Dutch term *dichten*, to compose poetry, originates from the word *dicht*, which means condensed or tight. In this view, the creation of poetry therefore can be seen as a process of condensing or "compacting" thought and its forms of expression. And, generally speaking, poems are indeed much shorter and more compact than prose pieces, which convey happenings in lengthy detail.

In the creation of poetry, a distillation of thought and experience takes place; more often than not what underlies poems are philosophical conclusions. The tendency (on the part of the poet) to philosophize is apparent in even the simplest of poems. Though rarely are the poems of adolescents real literature, nonetheless they often do pulsate with moans, cries, and whispers about life's suffering. But here the writer's point of view or his understanding of life is rarely supported by substantial or deeply-felt experience. Even so, one must admit, the tendency of such poems to philosophize remains.

At the very least, poems attempt to express the human predicament, regardless of whether the unfortunate fate is that of the poet himself or of man in general. In the latter instance, the suffering of humanity is *weltschmerz*, the world's pain. The "I" in such poems must in fact be interpreted as "we."

If Sutardji Calzoum Bachri in his poems asks "How can a poet reach God when words are unable," his cry of longing for God emerges not only from his soul, but from the soul of every man who wants to be closer to God yet feels impotent, for his words do not have the power to reach Him. That it is not only the poet himself who feels his words are impotent is shown in the poem "Kalian," meaning "you" in the inclusive sense. This poem has only one word, that being *"pun,"* which means "too" or "even." In reading Sutardji's poems we, too, begin to think more deeply about the essence of both words and God and, as this poet did in his collection of verse entitled *Oh Amuk Kapak* (*Oh Amuck Axe*), will also wail from the loss of hope of finding God. All that we find is loneliness and cynicism. The futility of attempting to reach God and the loss of trust in words to speak to God is the major philosophical theme of Sutardji's poetry.

The closeness of philosophy and poetry can also be seen in the poetry of Sapardi Djoko Damono, in particular in his collection of poems entitled *Mata Pisau* (*Blade*). Both the philosopher and the poet view life as a problem, as a puzzle to be solved. But whereas the philosopher, relying on the power of a rigid system of thought, would try to wrest the answer from the secretive maze, the poet produces only questions. Nonetheless, precisely because of his questioning, the possibility of an answer appears both alluring and inviting, quite outside of frozen dogmatic concepts, and arising in us, the readers, who also ask.

In his poems, Sapardi asks such questions as "Where do we come from?," "Who are we?" and "Where are we going?" – a set of basic philosophical questions.

Sapardi frequently asks "Where are you taking me, my friend?" and "Where have the birds flown?" The secret meaning of life's journey is stated by the poet in the words: "We travel searching for the border of morning's fog..." and in "And then I journeyed half-asleep through the air growing thicker with smoke..." The high incidence of rain in Sapardi's poems raises images of both the mystery of life and the anxiousness of the poet in attempting to express life's meaning.

More biting are the questions that arise from doubts about the meaning of life and self-identity. These questions, too, form another basic philosophical theme. "Who is man?" Sapardi asks repeatedly. "What is your name?," he asks in the poem "Narcissus." Man's aversion to looking at his own face often raises false assumptions: "I am the water...am seaweed am mud am air bubbles am glass am..."

As can be seen in the book-length poem *Pengakuan Pariyem (Pariyem's Confession)* by Linus Suryadi, a poet's worldview might just as well *not* be based on personal views and experience, but on the accepted views of a particular social group instead. The major character in *Pariyem* is Maria Magdalena Pariyem, a young woman from the village of Wonosari at the foot of Mount Kidul who works as a servant for the blue-blooded Cokrosentono family in Yogyakarta, Central Java. Unlike the Mary Magdalene of the Bible who is aware of and regrets her sin, Maria Magdalena from Wonosari is blithely unaware of sin. Pariyem is much more Javanese than Catholic. "If one is a true Javanese," she says, "it is unnecessary to ask about sin." Pariyem's beliefs and world view are rooted in the Javanese philosophy of life, which she encapsulates in the words, "For a long and fruitful life, life must be harmonious with nature." Her guideline for life is that one be able to recognize both "limitations and constraints," that one both think and feel *sak madya*, that is to be moderate, not excessive. Pariyem is *lil-legawa*, patient and accepting; she maintains a willingness to accept whatever kind of life fate presents her. In more concrete terms, she is willing to accept her life as a servant because nature's law has determined that there are priyayi, those who are to be served, and there are those who must serve, and the two are inseparable.

Through Pariyem, Linus expounds on *ngelmu krasan*, the knowledge or philosophy of accommodation. Through her as well, the poet implies that culture must adhere to this same principle (*krasan*) and to the spiritual bond that exists between oneself and one's traditions and country. This is a cultural view that is very much in conflict with the principle of universalism that was followed by Indonesian poets of a previous generation, such as Chairil Anwar and Sitor Situmorang. In *Pariyem* such people are "people with the souls of wanderers, forever in search of an anchor in another world, foreigners in their own land, distant and unfriendly."

This description of the attitude of the previous generation of poets, especially if applied to Chairil Anwar and Sitor Situmorang, seems particularly accurate. In comparing the poetry of Sutardji Calzoum Bachri, Sapardi Djoko Damono, and Linus Suryadi with that of Chairil Anwar and Sitor Situmorang, there is indeed a marked difference in cultural atmosphere and orientation. In the poetry of the three later poets one senses an intimate relationship between the poets themselves and the problems of their own world, regardless of whether those problems are personal in nature or affecting the Indonesian people as a whole. In Chairil and Sitor's poems the reader finds more abstract problems of life and culture. These two poets wrestle with ideas that are rooted in the philosophical views of foreign lands, especially Europe.

When entering the world of poetry created by Chairil Anwar and Sitor Situmorang, one seems to leave one's own world. Their poems do indeed evoke the image of a human spirit with roots upturned, bringing with them the flavor of Western intellectual thought.

Chairil, in his poems, fights and wrestles, trying to free himself from the grasp of his own land. He gives all his strength "to seeking the greenness of another sea." He feels alienated from the world around him. "Fate is separate loneliness-es," he says in his poem "Pemberian Tahu (Announcement)." "Don't tie your life to mine. I can't be with anyone for long. This, too, I write on a ship, on some nameless sea." The poet is forever belayed by longing in settings far from his own homeland. Chairil's flight from the embrace of women on land often leads him to a dead end, to a vacuum of values and to nihilism. "It is so very late. All meaning is drowned, and motion has no meaning," he says in "Kawanku dan Aku (My Friend and I)."

The poet Chairil Anwar quite consciously severed his roots from his own land: He thought himself to have a European soul, to hail from a culture which he in fact never once visited and knew only in the abstract. In this search for abstract values the result – in most of his poems – was a certain tension and anxiousness. At the same time, one also finds in his poems a certain machismo, a lust for vitalism, a life force whose inspiration he obtained from the Dutch poet Marsman. Can we possibly say that the alienation Chairil felt towards his own world and culture was perhaps that awareness of life found in existentialist thought? As if molded by the tone of heroism found in Jean-Paul Sartre's writings, Chairil, too, attempted to present himself as a character of strength, a virile and carefree man.

In the late 1940s and early 1950s, the period in which Chairil and Sitor Situmorang first made their mark as poets, existentialism was in fact a favored topic of discussion and object of study among Indonesia's cultural and literary elite. If elements of existentialism appear like flashes in the poems of Chairil Anwar (who wrote in the 1940s), existentialism becomes a beacon in the writings of Sitor Situmorang, especially so in one of his dramas, *Jalan Mutiara (Road of Pearls)*.

Sitor creates an intellectual atmosphere very much in keeping with that suggested by Sartre and Camus. In *Road of Pearls*, the concepts of these two French existentialists, fuse and meld. The play puts a marked stress on individual responsibility and freedom of choice, one of Sartre's favorite themes. This is echoed in the words of one of the play's characters: "...my stance, which you have always thought to be cynical or fatalistic, is resolute: to make one's own decisions, free from the influence of others, free from public morals and opinion, to take responsibility for one's own actions in this life... That is the one and only justification for this drama that drags us down. Make a decision! But whatever decision you make, carry it out with awareness, for that is the challenge that fate presents."

This same character presents Camus' view on suicide as a means to overcome the absurdity or meaningless of life: "...the point is, suicide is a challenge to fate. If it is not in one's power to avert one's birth or one's presence in this world, then the only freedom that is left to us is the freedom to end one's own life."

Further, in Sitor's poems, the word *iseng* appears frequently and is very close in meaning to Sartre's much-used term *la nausee*. Though often translated as "nausea," the term also defines the "butterflies" an artist might feel in creating something.

Three collections of poems by Sitor Situmorang, *Surat Kertas Hijau (Green Paper Poems)*, *Dalam Sajak (In Poetry)*, and *Wajah Tak Bernama (The Nameless Face)*, repeat, with little variation among them, the theme of the poet's self alienation, not only from his friends, his country, and his people, but also from God. The poet, at least at the time he wrote these poems, was indeed an alienated man grasping for a bond between himself and the world outside. His efforts were futile. His poems show the alienation experienced by the poet in attempting to adjust his views on life with existentialism.

IN THIS BRIEF DISCUSSION, I have avoided revealing details or nuances in the development of the assortment of the aforementioned poems because the point of this discussion is the link between philosophy and poetry. In the poetic output of the poets there is an invisible thread that not only connects one poem with another, but also leads one to the basic philosophical premises that underline these poets' views.

Their poems might speak of longing for something distant, for the sea, for a lover, or for God. This is a symptom of the romantic, an attempt to distance oneself from reality. But the theme of alienation, including alienation from oneself and loss of trust in one's identity, is also deeply etched in these writers' poems, so very much so that we cannot help but see their poems as philosophical expressions of the attitudes and views of life that mark the culture of their time. With the exception of Linus Suryadi, whose works both balance and contrast quite strikingly with those of the other poets, all of the poets discussed show a marked trend towards existentialist philosophy.

The reason behind this is, I suspect, that the various currents of existentialism, as with literature, touch not only on the intellectual side of man but are much more tightly connected with the totality of man. By necessity philosophy is concerned with man, said Heinemann: "It should be an expression of the whole man and not merely his intellect." And as it is with existentialism, so it is with literature, and poetry in particular. Poetry today is literature of crisis, revelations of life's struggle wherein values are changing and trust in fate and God is shaky. Thus it is that we find in poetry the same kind of themes or problems of life that are found in existentialism which is, in itself, a mark of philosophical crisis. Alienation and the absurdity of life, in particular, are themes peculiar to contemporary philosophy and poetry.

Another reason behind the close link between existentialism and poetry is the philosophical view that life "cannot be systematized." We find this in poetry as well. In poetry, we see a resolution of this existentialist idea but in a written form, one that is without a "scientific" system, yet is nonetheless capable of capturing and expressing the meaning of life.

1989

TRANSLATED BY JOHN H. MCGLYNN

Sources:

Heidegger, Martin: *Poetry, Language, Thought* (translation with introduction by Albert Hofstatter); Harper & Row, New York, 1975.

Maritain, Jaques: *Creative Intuition in Art and Poetry*, Pantheon Books, New York, 1960.

Heinemann, F.H.: *Existentialism and the Modern Predicament;* Harper & Brother, New York, 1958.

Read, Herbert: *English Prose Style*, Beacon Press, 1955.

CHAIRIL ANWAR

My Friend and I

for L.K. Bohang

we share the same path. Late at night
Penetrating fog
Rain drenching our bodies

Ships freeze in the harbor.

My blood curdles. My mind congeals.

Who's speaks?
My friend is but a skeleton
Scourged of his strength.

He asks the time!

It is so late
All meaning has sunk and drowned
And motion has no purpose.

1943

No, Woman!

No, woman! What lives in me
still easily evades your fevered and dark embrace,
intent on finding the greenness of another sea,
to be again on the ship where we first met,
surrendering the rudder to the wind,
our eyes fixed on waiting stars.
Something flapping its wings, again conveys
Tai Po and the secrets of the Ambonese sea
Such is woman! A single vague line
is all I can write
in my flight towards her enigmatic smile.

1945

Announcement

To dictate fate is not my intent,
fate is separate loneliness-es.
I choose you from among the rest, but
in a moment we are snared by loneliness once more.
There was a time I really wanted you,
to be as children in crowning darkness,
we kissed and fondled, not tiring
I did not want to ever let you go.
Do not unite your life with mine,
I can not be with anyone for very long
I write this now on a ship, in some nameless sea.

1946

Pines in the Distance

Pines scatter in the distance,
as day becomes night,
branches slap weakly at the window,
pushed by a sultry wind.

I'm now a person who can survive,
so long ago I left childhood behind,
though once there was something,
that now counts for nothing at all.

Life is but postponement of defeat,
a growing estrangement from youth's unfettered love
knowing there's always something left unsaid
before we finally acquiesce.

1949

That Night We Were There

"excuse me, but why did you bring me here?", a station
at night's end. White shadows at the platform's end
trace the long benches; the clock's hands, leaping
untiringly cling fast to Silence. It just might be

we are waiting for the train that usually arrives
whenever no one is ready to give the signal,
or we just might want to be here
when no one is hurrying about, waiting, disappointed

our sighs alone, tracing the ties, suddenly stiffen;
signals freeze, yellow lamps fade in midair;
as white shadows fill the entire room: "But, please
tell me first, why did you bring me here?"

1970

On the Veranda When it Rains

You call your memory song (and not the sun
that stirs the dust on the road, enhancing
the colors of flower garlands, that erase
footsteps, that go on forever
in the rain. And you, on the veranda
alone, "The birds... (which I, in fact
have never seen, transform into a kind of song,
a kind of stillness) where have they flown? And where is the woosh
     of the leaves
that twirl far into every dream?"

(It is not the dry season that exudes the sky,
that slowly settles in the air) you call your love
a long rain, constantly
clearing the dust, that sings in the garden.
On the veranda, you sit
alone, "And where are the swarms of butterflies,
that evade my vision; and where is
(oh, no!) my forming longing?"

And you, on the veranda, hear but do not hear
the rain, alone,
"Where is heaven: the song
they once taught me, word by word
I learned to recite
even in my sleep?" And you call your life
evening (and not midday
that breathes heavily,
suddenly hardens beneath the sun) wet,
melting in the waves of rain,
dissolving.

Amen.

1970

Narcissus

and just like me: what is your name, is it not so?
on the pool's surface your features are calm; within, your longing
    deep
but let us not fall in love
there is no need to reach you, for you change into me

or to wait until the wind loosens a leaf
that falls into the pool: your mien pulsates, does it not?
will I be disappointed if the pool grows calm again?
will I be disappointed if all the leaves, one after another, fall

1971

Journey

then I half-dreaming journied through air that grew ever more
     thick with smoke
(the pools of silt and gold fish were still tucked neatly away in the
     palms of my hands)
counting electric poles of twelve different colors!
"who said that shards of steel are scattered about in the chant of a
     grandmother's lullabye?"

1973

Aquarium

it's you who said it: her eyes are like a fish!
it's you who said it: her eyes and hair and shoulders like a fish!
it's you who said it: her eyes and hair and shoulders and arms and
       chest and waist and thighs like a fish!
"I am water!" you screamed, "I am mud, and moss, and bubbles,
       and glass, and..."

1973

Cathèdrale de Chartres

Will He speak in the silent night
When falling snow and birds are pure white
At times he wished to surrender his heart
To the refuge of pure devotion

Oh, God, we can not meet again
In prayer with the convocation
In the eyes of a mute lover I take my love
Life is inseparable from doom

She sobbed in tears on Easter day
On our visit to the Chartres Cathedral
Her prayers somber beneath the colors of stained glass
Christ was crucified by man, what else is there to say

And on that night before the cock crowed
And the people of Chartres had quit their revelry
She sobbed amid night's falling leaves
Her memory roaming the drizzling rain

For my mother, my wife, my children and Jesus
My heart is cleft by adultery and devotion
I have but one love, there is but one God
Life and doom walk hand in hand

Such is the story of our love
That began at the flower market
In the early hours of morn near Notre Dame de Paris
In the season of flowers and downcast eyes

Such is the story of Easter day
When all of nature was pursued by unease
By tempatation, adultery, love and the city
For her, for me and for my faithful wife

And so that night to the hostel's bed
Came the holiness of a church song
Together with God's curse of passion and grace
Beckoning faithfulness and a woman's embrace

And so it is
An Easter tale
A time of damp earth
And restless tears
Flowers in bloom
On French soil
On Fragrant earth
When Christ was crucified

1953

A Poem

Why not believe in God?
Such sadness is poetry

On us he has no hold
In sorrow only does he stir

In our death
He too is stropped by silence

1953

La Ronde, I

Humming in the forgetfulness of his encounter
with the night, he's alone in the room.
The season climbs until the snow
and falls as hunger grows

Two memories, disembodied–
The smells of their presence intertwine:
"Oh, to die like this," comes a dark whisper
From the peak of pleasure, until dawn

Lying on night's breast. "You're all mine,"
gasping moments flow into kisses,
frenzied lips search for time
and solidify in the woman's body

The season climbs until the dawn
Outside the open window, falling snow.

1955

Morning Field

in Sukabumi

In front of the inn is a stand of pines,
Fowers and an empty field
In back, a lane leads to the river.
And further back, a highway to the city.

Morning clouds hang on the distant slope
Children come to the field to play ball,
The sun rises to brighten the sky,
Reverberant laughter and cheers.

As far as the eye can see, only mountains
As far as daydreams roam, only green
I guess I was asleep, I guess it was a dream,
Roused from an endless sleep.

The bell in the barracks near by rings shrill:
One o'clock – half the day is gone.
Now the room is very light
But the field out there is silent.

I shiver. In a corner I didn't suspect
Night's cold lingers still.

1955

Pilgrimage to a Mountain Church

Wherever I am you are there
The one and only image
Are you really here in this silence
In the chill of this lonely church?

From outside, into this room
Comes the trill of a bird in praise of morning
While I am here, just me alone
With a chill the sun will never warm.

Amen.

Leaf

leaf

bird

river

quiver

hoping   reach   sky

who   knows

fruit   grass   blanket

chest   blue

sky   dice

come!

grass   blade   stone   you

you   you   you   you   you   you   you

you   you   you YOU   you   you   you

you   you   you   you   you   you   you

you

1970

Becomes

not every ache
                becomes a wound
not every silence
                becomes a thorn
not every symbol
                becomes intent
not every question
                becomes equivocation
not every answer
                becomes rationale
not every urge
                becomes desire
not every hand
                becomes a grip
not every word
                becomes learning
not every wound
                becomes a mirror
                        in which to see You
                                in my face!

1972

what flows

what flows? blood. what blooms? roses. what swells? hope. what feels? regret. with a thousand regrets I search for You with all means available I search for you with a thousands contrivances I search for you with a thousand temptations I search for You

1973

Even

the poet, however great
will not reach allah's bounds

I once invited god
into myself
but not now

in death
when my death might be but an end post
but the final grain of sand
spirit becomes ascendent in verse

with seven peaks counting
day's dazzle disclosing
I write of my longing on grains of sand

even with all the letters, each and every one used
my ABCs do not reach allah's bounds

1979

Pariyem's Confession

(Excerpts from a Prose Poem)

Pariyem's my name
Born in Wonosari, Gunung Kidul, on the island of Java
But I work in the inland-city of Ngayogyakarta
I am 25 years old
– but forgive me
I forget the date of my birth
The *weton* however I know well
The *wuku* of Kuningan
under the protection of the Lord Indra,
The day, Friday *Wage'*
just as dawn was breaking

Pariyem I am, Pariyem
born on a bench with a mat for a mattress
together with my placenta
Cut apart by the midwife, with a bamboo knife
seven times sharper than a barber's blade
My younger-sister placenta was mixed
with raw egg, uncooked rice, coins,

onion, garlic, sugar, salt, ginger and *kencur*
Then cleaned and placed in an earthenware pot
and buried in front of the house
That's right, eggs: a symbol of the newborn babe
innocent, pure
turning and squirming, helpless
Rice and coins: symbols of hope
that life will be without want
of clothing, food and money
Onions and garlic, sugar, salt, ginger and *kencur;*
symbols of the bitter-sweetness of life
that lies ahead, and so
not to be too sad in sorrow
not to be too happy in happiness
And with a simple ceremony the placenta is buried
to the right of the front door if the baby is a boy
to the left of the front door if the baby is a girl
A burning torch marks the place
until the baby is thirty-five days old

Pariyem I am, Pariyem
My father says this name brings good luck
And after five days, one *pasaran* as we say,
so he named me
And a mat was laid with food on the earthen floor:
Red rice-porridge: a sign of the purity of the newborn babe
White rice-porridge: a sign of the light that brightens nature
stuffed whole chicken: a sign of the wholeness of body and soul
            lying naked
A rice-mountain and green-leaf vegetables:
            to show the friendships of life
that lie ahead to enrich us

Coconut-flavored porridge: a sign of hope –
hope that the sinews and muscles of the mother
will soon be strong again as before
And the newborn baby will be ever so strong and healthy.
For the *kenduri* ceremony
the neighbors come from the whole village
– sitting in a circle on mats on the floor
Pak Kaum leads the prayers
Prayers for the well-being of the mother just given birth
and prayers for the well-being of the newborn baby
To the Lord of All Things, we offer thanks
with praise we pray
We hope the arrival of this baby is blessed by all
and by all of nature and all that nature holds
And so a new creature is added to this earth
Next morning is the children's ceremony
and mother gives the children gifts of food
So that sickness and misfortune will be kept at bay
vanish, depart from my existence

Pariyem, yes Pariyem
From *"Pari"* meaning young riceplant
After all, my father was a farmer
But he only worked a small plot
given him in return for village work
not big at all
Just three small patches
beside the river
to feed all of us
a family of five
I am the oldest
I have a younger brother and sister

Pairin works at home, weaving rattan hats
Painem helps mother at the market
And father works each day in the rice fields
laboring, tilling the soil

●

The early morning sun spreads its rays
The world of Ngayogyakarta is freed from darkness
And the flowers open
and birds take to flight
The day resounds in a flood of light
everything following the rhythm of nature

I've been wondering
I've been thinking
Life's not to be thought about
life's not to be pondered over
From beginning to end
life is flowing
As the Winanga River
as the Codhé, in the middle of town,
as the Gadjah Wong
Our lives are flowing
While prices rise
– soaring wildly
the price of rice never keeps up
Harvest is just once each six months
maybe three or four times a year with PB or IR seed
Sure, sure, everything depends on the harvest,
from the harvest all else follows
This is absurd, impossible,

Doesn't make sense. How can it?
For mouths still open wide
and each day stomachs still ask to be fed
For every single need
the harvest is our backbone
We live by digging holes and filling them again
never free from debt
But don't we live in a community
with our neighbors all around?
Together with them we share the burden
But not because of cooperation
not as a shared lottery
But because we are in each other's debt
enclosed in good-neighborliness
Yes, all depends on the harvest
And our life flows on
the years eat away, the world keeps watch
And we at the center of reality
we faithful, in the middle together
follow along in the current of life
And our life flows on
from the source, from the spring
all of us are flowing
Appearing from the source of darkness
lost in the darkness of the spring:
this is the ancient riddle
the end of the ocean of life
And life flows on
And so it is with me;
I, like the river Winangka
I, like the Codhé River in the middle of town
I, like the Gajah Wong River

From my birth until this moment
I too am flowing

●

Pariyem, yes, Pariyem
or "Iyem" for everyday
I grew big and strong
My body blossomed as Father had wished
my body blossomed as nature designed
And I grew even bigger
Until the young men in Yogya would taunt me
and often tease me
I grew chubby
My body grew a bit fat
But, so what
I don't care
so be it

●

I am spinning a thread
I am telling of a memory long passed
Like water in a pool: flowing to the edge
Clean, calm and still
leaves held floating on the surface

It was late at night
We were going home from watching a shadow play
The puppeteer was Kimpul from Sleman
and he performed "The Kidnapping of Sukesi"
And mother, as the singer, would remain until dawn
one of the men then walking her home

My father was in a *ketoprak* troupe in Tempel
he used to come home once a week
And the *gamelan* was lively
loud, fast
Playing in a *slendro-sanga* mode
a sign that the *gara-gara* had begun
And the moon was leaning to the west
a sign it would soon be daybreak
We wove our way along the path
– the grass cold, wet with dew
nature white, covered with mist
And we nibbled on sweet cassava and peanuts
walking hand-in-hand
We felt the cold night breeze in our bones
the cold making us shiver
We passed the village of Karang
Wonosari lay before us
We went on, halfway there, strolling along
and I wrapped my sash around my neck
And he held my hand tightly
and I held his hand tightly
And oh, I was drawn to the shelter
the harvesters' rest-place in the hot midday sun
I didn't know what he was taking me there for
but my instinct told me
Suddenly I could not speak, full of doubt
but my blood pulsed, urging me on
My heart throbbed, beating loudly
I no longer knew what was happening
He took off his jacket, his *sarong*, his underpants
he took off my blouse, my *sarong*, my bodice
Oh, God, Lord forgive me

173

there we were, completely naked!
And he kissed my lips
their first kiss from a man
And he nibbled my earlobes
their first nibbling from a man
Oh God, how ticklish it was
all the hairs on the back of my neck were tingling
– on edge
And he rubbed my thighs
their first rub from a man
And he squeezed my hips
their first squeeze from a man
And he licked my belly-button
its first licking from a man
Oh God, and the world went completely black
My breath panting wildly
my blood rushing madly
And then, ask no more –
He rode me like a horse
threw himself down and upon me
And my body was pierced through and through

Bumi gonjang	The earth moves
langit ganjing	the sky shakes
Bumi dan langit	Earth and sky
gonjang ganjing	quaking, shaking

United in frenzy
we were given blessing
And he whispered in my left ear
a Javanese secret

O rasaku, o ragamu   Oh you and I
dudu mungsuh dudu satru   neither enemy nor foe
Jagad wadonmu,   Your womanness,
jagad lanagku   my manness
ngrasuk rasa   penetrating being,
ngrasuk kalbu   penetrating soul

Over and over he whispered
Over and over he stabbed
as a *kris* blade enters its sheath
and so it is for men and women
And then suddenly I had to pee
I just couldn't hold it back
He called me "Iyem"
I called him "Kliwon"
Oh we moved as one in our lovemaking
And then we lay next to each other
thrown side-by-side
Our bodies limp, with no strength left
as though we had just feasted –
Without speaking, without a sound
overflowing with feeling; There could be no words
Just the night breeze rustling
and our panting breath
The moon and the stars
all kinds of crickets and locusts
and other sounds of nature
laid bare: the mist was clearing
The *gamelan* orchestra played a battle scene
two heroes on the battlefield
The puppeteer's song, waves
piercing the stillness of the night

echoes slicing the darkness
waves in the stillness
Oh father, oh mother
your daughter is no longer a virgin
And he stroked my hair
its first stroking by a man
And he kissed my forehead
its first kiss by a man
And he took me on his knee
my first embrace by a man
Ouch! Ants were biting my thighs
– and we quickly got ready
Both of us hurriedly getting dressed
as though suddenly surrounded by a crowd
A new mood, a new urgency
struggling to take over in the soul
Oh God, Lord have mercy
I felt prickly all over
We had made love near an ant's nest
on top of a pile of dried rice husks

I walked home a bit wobbly
while I brushed the dirt off my sash
leaning on Kliwon's shoulder
I had a feeling of peace
Oh, this memory of memories
we had etched out to the deepest detail

1980

TRANSLATED BY JENNIFER LINDSAY

Glossary:

gara-gara: Central section of the all-night shadow puppet play lasting from around 1:00 AM to 3:330 AM when the world is shown in a state of tumult.

pasaran: one five-day cycle made up of five *pasar* or market days

slendro-sanga: "*Sanga*" is one of three modes in the five-tone tuning system called "*slendro*".

Wage': one of the days in the Jayanese five-day week.

weton: a Javanese term referring to the combination of days from the five and seven-day week cycles that falls on the day of one's birth. This combination, together with the *wuku*, is believed to influence every aspect of one's life.

wuku: A seven-day division in the Javanese calendrical system from the cycle of 210 days which is divided into thirty *wuku*.

Blood

WHILE SLICING ONIONS, Mirah cut her finger. She cried out and popped her index finger into her mouth. But, startled, she pulled it out again. Her wet finger was pale. Blood was rushing into the cut and dripping down. Mirah was stunned: the blood was white.

In the tales of the shadow theater the only character with white blood was Prince Yudhistira, the eldest child of the Pandawa family and a hero with a pure heart. His blood was not only a symbol of his majesty but also a guarantee that he would enter heaven as soon as he died. Because he eschewed violence in all his actions and because he was always willing to make sacrifices for others, Yudhistira had been blessed with white blood.

But Mirah was not a *wayang* heroine. She lived in a large city in which the most important thing – although many people did not agree with this – was money, money, money.

Mirah didn't believe it. She looked away, trying to clear her head; but when she looked again, the blood on her index finger was still white, clear, fresh and fragrant. It had a healthy smell, like the smell of the earth during rain. Only its taste was bitter.

Mirah was confused. She felt neither headachy nor nauseous; in fact, she felt very good. Never before had anyone felt so refreshed while losing blood. This was like the Dracula film which she had seen not long ago.

Mirah held her finger to a cup to catch the blood. It flowed cheerfully and playfully down her finger. Like a child who had been kept inside too long, it burst from Mirah's finger and fell into the cup – drip, drip, drip. Her index finger no longer felt like a part of her own hand. It had become part of Yudhistira's hand. Enveloped in wonder, Mirah prayed. She did not understand why she had been chosen for this miracle.

There are many people more learned than I, she thought. Some neighbors have BAs. Some are even lecturers. Why have I been chosen, she wondered. I, who only went to elementary school?

Mirah thought of her mother and father who had died long ago, murdered. And now here she was: the only person with white blood among millions and millions of people with red blood. What was this if not amazing? She would be famous. She would have lots of money. Because of this, she would be rich! She would move to a house of her own. She would no longer have to live in her aunt's house and be pushed around all her life.

Mirah could hardly breathe. She was happy. The cup was filling up. Quickly she looked for a glass. Suddenly her aunt came in. Startled, Mirah picked up the cup and drank up all her blood. Then she put her injured finger back into her mouth.

"What's the matter, Mirah? Why do you have your finger in your mouth?"

Mirah did not answer.

"Well, what's the matter?" her aunt asked.

"Nothing."

"Nothing? But you're sucking your finger like an imbecile. Did you cut yourself?"

"No."

"Work a little faster. Just slicing those onions has taken you hours! Look at that room. Don't let the dirty clothes pile up like that!"

"I'll wash them later," Mirah told her aunt.

"There are two baskets full now, and how they smell! And when you're finished with the laundry, clean the store room. Did you hear me, Mirah?"

"Yes."

"After that you can take over for me in the shop. There's a club meeting at Mrs. Daniel's house."

Mirah nodded in assent.

She has been holding her index finger tightly, but as soon as her aunt left the kitchen, she stuck it into the cup again. The blood welled out again, slick and lively, white and clean like the sap of the frangipani tree. For the first time in her twenty years Mirah felt that life was good and worthwhile. Tears fell from her eyes, as the faces of her father and mother again floated hazily before her. How difficult it was to be alone in this hectic world. But now, because of her white blood everything was going to be different. Mirah smiled.

Cheerfully, nimbly, she on light steps to the well. She attacked her two baskets of laundry and took care of the washing in two hours, all the while singing pop songs. After that she invaded the storage room. Full of energy she went after the dirt; drenched in sweat, she made the storeroom shine.

The entire house was in an uproar. Her aunt and uncle were amazed. For twenty years they had thought of Mirah as a dark, impenetrable hole. The orphaned girl had been like a mask, closed against the whole world. Only now, suddenly, Mirah had begun to show the emotions of a normal person.

"I like you this way. I hope you can stay like this," her aunt said, offering her a steamed dumpling.

Her uncle praised her: "You're grown up now, Mirah. Now you

understand that to become somebody, you have to work hard. The harder you work, the better a person you will be. Life is difficult and if you don't work, you don't eat. It is a good thing, Mirah, that you are beginning to understand that what we've been teaching you has been for the good of your own future."

Mirah was embarrassed; her aunt and uncle's praise made her proud. All she had ever heard before was that she was rotten. Her relationship with her adoptive parents had not been good. They had always treated her like some sort of alien. She had been trained to work hard and control her feelings to enable her to face a difficult future. As a result she had never felt part of the household, but only like some sort of hand-me-down.

But now all that had changed. She didn't care any more. It didn't matter if the others didn't think of her as a relative; it didn't matter that she was alone in the world. It didn't matter that her father and mother had turned to dust long ago and that they were still spoken of badly. She still had something to be proud of. She had something to believe in. And soon other people would know that, except for Yudhistira, she was the only person to have white blood. She smiled to herself.

Mirah kept on smiling through the evening.

That night, for the first time, she was invited to eat with the other members of the household. Her aunt and uncle looked at her again and again, amazed.

"It looks like you're beginning to show some understanding," her aunt said with apparent emotion.

Mirah lowered her head.

Her aunt went on. "And we're happy, too, Mirah, that you're beginning to realize how things are in life: That you've got to make an effort, to make something of your life."

Mirah only smiled, not wanting to explain just yet what had happened. She wanted to savor her happiness alone. Later, in front of the television she laughed at the antics of the Srimulat comedians. Her aunt leaned toward her and stroked her hair. "Praise God," she cried. "After all these years, you've finally grown up. You've changed! This is our reward for being patient," the woman said as she continued to stroke her niece's hair.

"You see now, don't you," her uncle continued, "that your aunt's harshness and her demands have really been due to her love and affection for you. Twenty years, your aunt has taken care of you, Mirah. For twenty years she was unable to touch your heart. It seemed to have turned to stone. Your aunt has tried her best to think of you as one of her own. But you've always resisted. You've been wild and stubborn, always blaming others. Thank God, everything has changed. It isn't too late, after all. We'll hold a *selamatan* tomorrow and have yellow rice to celebrate."

Mirah nodded.

Her aunt sobbed. "You finally realize that we love you," she whispered. "This means that goodness does have a use. Isn't it right what I said before? You can't stop loving someone; because love takes time. You have to practice to love and be loved. Everything needs patience. Especially love! But why has it taken so long? Why didn't you realize this a long time ago?"

Mirah said nothing. She carried the words of her aunt and uncle with her to her room. But after lying down for a while, she began to want to share her happiness. The truth which had only just forced its way out into the open, was thrashing about wanting to be made known to others, before it disappeared in a rush. "Oh, I hope that all this isn't just a dream!" she whispered to herself. "It's better to tell it now, before it is lost."

Not caring that it was already midnight, Mirah knocked on the door to her aunt's room. Her aunt and uncle rose at once to find out what she wanted.

Mirah didn't know how to start. Again and again she took a deep breath, but still she couldn't explain. Her throat seemed constricted.

Her aunt patted her back and stroked her brow. Her uncle went to fetch some water. Mirah's step brothers and sisters were also awake and now watched from a distance.

"Drink this first."

Mirah drank the water her uncle had brought her.

"Are you sick?"

Mirah shook her head. She led her adoptive parents to the kitchen. She picked up the cup she had used to catch her blood. At last she was able to talk, but her voice sounded forced.

"When I was peeling onions this morning, I cut my finger." Mirah showed her aunt her left hand. "And I was shocked, because the blood that flowed from the cut in my finger was white. I caught it in this cup. My blood has always been red – but now it's white! I couldn't believe it. So I cut my finger a little more, to make sure whether my blood was really white. Why is it white, and not red, like other people's? Here, see for yourself." Mirah held the cup out to her aunt. "Why is my blood white?"

Mirah's uncle and aunt stared at the cup and then at her bandaged index finger. The other children pressed around, hoping to see the white blood. Everyone seemed puzzled.

"So, I'm sorry," Mirah continued, "but because my hand is hurt, I won't be able to work in the kitchen tomorrow. And I won't be able to do laundry or clean the storeroom. I can only help with going to the market and with taking care of the shop. That's how it has to be," she said to her aunt. "After all, with this cut in my hand, how can I work with only one hand?"

Mirah put out her hand. Her aunt and uncle just stared at it until, finally, it seemed they had grasped Mirah's message. They nodded, then sent Mirah back to her room.

"Sure, starting tomorrow you don't have to do the laundry," her Aunt said coldly. "Iyem can do everything. You don't have to do laundry any more, and you don't have to sweep, either. Let Iyem do it all. You just go to the market and do the shopping and after that you can mind the shop."

Mirah thanked her aunt for her understanding and went to her room. Her adoptive parents remained standing in place, staring after her.

"She's not a little girl any longer," Mirah's uncle suggested, "And even though she hasn't had much of an education, she is a young woman now. Maybe she's embarrassed to be told to do the laundry and other rough work."

Mirah's aunt didn't answer. A sour look grew on her face and she began to groan as though she were about to die. In a panic her husband quickly fetched the mentholated balsam. He massaged her back with the balsem, then scraped it with a coin until it was hot and covered with welts. The children, in their own room, stayed up whispering until dawn.

When Mirah went to the market the next day, almost everyone stared at her. The news of her white blood had already spread by word of mouth. Several people asked her about it straight out.

"Is it true, Mirah?"

Mirah nodded.

"Is it white?"

"Yes."

"Not red?"

"No, white."

"Why is it white?"

"I don't know."

"How do you know it's white?"

"I saw it myself!"

"Are you kidding?"

Mirah smiled, which drove people to demand more answers. More and more of them gathered around. The security officer joined in the questioning. Then the police came, too, thinking there was a riot.

Worried and trying to avoid the commotion, Mirah hurried home.

But when she arrived at home, her aunt called her. "About your request last night..." the aunt began while trying to suppress her anger. "Don't get me wrong... Don't misunderstand but you can't go stirring up things left and right. If I've have always given you lots of work to do, it was to prepare you for life, to make you industrious, for your own future good. You know how to do laundry, how to wash floors, how to do housekeeping and kitchen chores. You can do any kind of work, now. And how did you get all these skills if not through practice? So don't think of this work as forced labor. It's an education, do you understand?"

Her uncle added: "We know what you're up to. But why do you have to make these insinuations? That's not good. Come out and tell us straight forward if something is wrong. If you don't like something, just say so, straight out. If you're tired, say so. Don't just keep quiet like an idiot. So, why all the hints all of a sudden? That's hard to accept. It's not good. After all, we've taken care of you for twenty years as though you were our own child. We didn't treat you any differently, did we? Tell me how we treated you differently? The rest of the kids had to work, too. There's no one here who doesn't work. So why are you ridiculing us like this? As of now – well, it's up to you. If you want to stay here, fine. If not, you can decide what you want. It's up to you. Your aunt and I have given up. We'll go along with whatever you want."

Mirah was growing confused.

Not long after, the security officer came to the house. He had been assigned to investigate further because the people at the market were in an uproar, saying that Mirah had white blood. "For our common peace of mind," he said politely, "I'd like you to come to the security post for a moment to clear things up."

At the security post Mirah was advised in earnest not to create any more unrest. "It's no good," the officer said with tremble in his voice.

"It makes us all uneasy."

Mirah nodded, meek and afraid. She looked around nervously, seeking help. Why were these people so upset just because she had white blood? "What did I do wrong?" Mirah cried.

"Never mind that. Now, the important thing, the most important thing to remember, is not to do it again. Okay?!"

"Alright."

"Well then, tell me again. What is it that you mustn't say?"

"I'm not to say that my blood is white. But my blood was white yesterday, I swear on my life!"

"There, you've done it again. Don't do that! You mustn't say that. Don't you understand?"

Mirah didn't understand but she nodded anyway.

"You are not to say that you have white blood. Do you understand?!"

"I was slicing onions when I cut my hand. The color of my blood was white, not red. I swear. Really, Mr. Jeki."

"Shhh! Stop! Keep quiet!"

Mirah didn't dare to speak again. She sat listening, without argument.

"Your blood is red. Everyone has red blood. Don't go stirring things up. Do you understand? Pretty soon someone else will come along and claim that his blood is red, white and blue. Then we'll have real trouble, won't we?"

"Yes, Mr. Jeki."

"Okay, you can go home now. But your blood is red, right?! Is it red or white?"

"It's red, Mr. Jeki."

"Good. You can go home now. Hmmm, now where's that piece of cake I was eating...?"

The officer escorted Mirah home and explained, or suggested, to her aunt and uncle that they keep a closer watch on her.

As soon as the man had gone, Mirah's aunt continued the scolding:

"Never before has this family had anything to do with the security officers, least not to the point where one has come here and questioned us. It's like we were thieves. This is too much, just too much! And all because of you and your nonsense, Mirah. If you just want to take it easy, if you don't want to work any more, you don't have to go around saying that you have white blood and other such nonsense. Next thing it will be black!"

"But it really was white, Aunt."

"Be quiet!"

"I swear it was white, really!"

"Shut up!"

Mirah walked away towards her room.

Her aunt screamed furiously, "If you do anything like this again, we'll send you to an orphanage. Or you can go to the village to live with your grandmother."

In her room Mirah tried to think, but her head hurt. What had gone wrong? In the end all she could do was stare. She stroked her finger as she listened to her aunt's voice vicious barrage which continued until night. She was afraid to leave the house. She was even afraid to move and so she stayed, standing in place, staring at her finger.

Not until sometime in the middle of the night, after everything had quieted down, did Mirah finally dare to move. And when she did she felt as though she had crawled out from under the rubble of a collapsed house.

Despite the attack she found that she was at peace, that her inner sense of happiness had not faded. She stared at her finger once more, as though she were gazing at a mine of truth. Now she had a friend. She felt a kind of yearning, an overpowering longing take hold of her. She shuddered. Maybe it was all a mistake. Maybe it was only her own fantasy. But she couldn't hold back the feeling: her happiness grew stronger, more real as it unfolded in her heart. The more she thought about what she possessed, the more invulnerable she felt.

She looked for a knife. In the drawer of the table she found a razor blade. Closing her eyes, Mirah tried to cut her finger; but it was difficult to do intentionally. She tried several times but failed. The blade slipped from her fingers and fell to the floor. Dazed, she quickly picked it up and in doing so she cut her hand again without meaning to.

Mirah hurried to get a glass to catch the blood. She prayed. "White, white, yes, Lord, let it be white," she whispered. It seemed forever before the blood began to ooze from the wound. Mirah stared at the cut. Once again she could not believe her eyes. She brought her hand close to the light bulb. Now she could see it clearly. The blood dripped into the glass – drip, drip, drip – and it was blue!

"Blue blood... No longer the blood of Yudhistira, but the blood of Prince Charles, the blood of kings, the blood of the aristocracy." Mirah whispered, with her eyes closed. "Not the blood of the common people at all."

She thought she could hear a Javanese song, the sound of a *gamelan* orchestra from she knew not where, accompanying the dripping of her blood. She heard admiring voices. Her body was no longer the body she had always known. Under the covering of her simple clothes, she felt a soft body, a noble body. In her breast she felt the beating of her heart, and knew it was not the heart of an ordinary person. Not the heart of a laundry woman, a sweeper, or a cook. Not the heart of a floor washer who could say nothing but "yes, yes, yes." Her heart was of pure gold, A heart of courage, accustomed to adoration, and to commanding other people.

As her blood dripped into the glass, Mirah slowly entered a world of her own. She became a queen. She became powerful. She was admired, honored, feared, respected, and loved by everyone. Her body exuded fragrance. The blood that flowed through her body radiated a blue light which cleansed her surroundings. She brought forth light, making everything glitter and become safe and prosperous.

When she awoke the next day, Mirah was determined and resolute.

No one else needed to know. It was enough to enjoy this happiness by herself. She took the shopping basket and went to her aunt.

"Hurry back and don't stop to chat," her aunt warned. "We're having a *selamatan* with yellow rice. The ceremony is for your own good, to keep you from being bothered by mischievous spirits."

Mirah nodded and immediately went on her way. But at the market everybody was already waiting for her. All of them: the meat seller, the vegetable seller, the ice seller, the meatball seller, the cigarette seller... All of them still wanted an explanation. Again she was mobbed with questions.

"I won't answer," Mirah whispered to herself. "I won't hear them. I won't talk to them."

But the more Mirah tried to avoid the people, the more they pressed for answers. They assaulted her with questions. Even one of the security officers assailed her. Finally Mirah plucked up the courage to speak.

"It's blue." she said.

The security officer was startled. "Blue, not white?"

"The day before yesterday it was white, but now it's blue," Mirah said proudly.

The people stared, open-mouthed. They gaped in disbelief. Faintly, from another part of the market, came the sound of a *dangdut* song sung by a roving singer. The crowd was dumbstruck and slowly began to move back, away from her. They couldn't comprehend the miracle. This was entirely strange. They looked at the orphaned girl with amazement.

Mirah felt touched by their display of emotion. She put down her shopping basket and hurried into the market, returning in no time from the direction of the meat seller. The people waited, wondering. Mirah's eyes gleamed with pride and happiness as she placed her left hand on top of the ice-storage container.

"See for yourselves, whether is it true or not?" Then, smiling

proudly, she raised her right hand and swiftly brought down the axe.
Crrruuunchhh!

1 9 8 7

TRANSLATED BY MILDRED L. E. WAGEMANN

The Gift

WIDI BECAME UNEASY every time New Year's rolled around. He couldn't help remembering the time thirty years ago when he was courting Maya. He had, with such passion and febrility, promised her a resplendent future. "I might be poor now, without a regular job, but my best point is that I believe in myself, and I am willing to work for a better future. I promise you that, at the very least, just for a change of pace, we will take a vacation to Singapore at the end of every year."

Maya, a pretty woman who had since become his wife, never actually believed him at the time. But because he repeated his blandishments so very often, she did eventually come to trust and believe in him. She, too, became sure that the will alone was enough to ensure their future, that the most ordinary of high school students could, if he were eager enough, produce all sorts of miracles.

After that time it became their wont to talk about what they would do supposing they really were able to take a vacation abroad every year.

They often imagined themselves as the kind of old tourists they saw at home, in Indonesia. Long before they married, they had daydreamed of seeing snow in Japan, of watching a "live show" in Bangkok, of visiting Disneyland in the United States, and so on and so forth. And, of course, they also imagined themselves strolling through the pulsating hubs of the world: Paris, New York, London and Rome, among others.

But now, after thirty years, their dreams had turned out to be only dreams. Widi had succeeded only in giving Maya several children. They had never even been to the nearby Puncak mountain resort for the weekend, much less Singapore. Were you to mention to Maya a few of Indonesia's better-known cities – Denpasar, Medan, or Ujung Pandang – she would tell you that she had never aspired to one day visit them. Try as he might, Widi was still no more than an ordinary office worker who was lucky just to be able to make ends meet. He was never able to set aside even a little extra so as to make the wheedling promises of his youth a reality.

Now that he was getting on in years, it seemed that he would have to be bury his former hopes once and for all. He had purchased lottery tickets several times, but then had stopped when finding it increasingly painful to face the future that stared at him each time he lost. He became ashamed and then depressed; he felt that he had failed as a paterfamilias, that he had failed as a man.

Maya never brought up Widi's youthful promises. Never again, that is, since the time she had made him cry. On that occasion, about five years earlier, as New Year's Eve approached, she had thought to sound him out, just for fun. "We've been married now for quite a few years, and New Year's is just around the corner. How about a little trip to Singapore?"

She had laughed when she said that but, much to her great surprise, her husband had just sat there, staring, absorbed in thought. He said nothing for such a long time that Maya began to get worried and immediately started talking about something else.

In the middle of that same night Widi had awoken. Maya, too. Their children were asleep. And Widi had begun to cry, blaming himself for his failure even as he begged Maya for her forgiveness.

Widi was torn up by remorse. "Forgive me, Maya," he had said, "I wasn't trying to trick you. I really did believe that I would be able to take you to Singapore. Singapore, heck! I was going to take you around the whole wide world. I swear to God, I was convinced that, with you at my side, I would some day be rich. I even thought – crazy, huh? – that we would own several villas abroad. But now, the way things turned out, as you well know, it hasn't been easy going. I guess where there's a will there isn't always a way. I just don't seem to have the luck that others have."

All Maya could do was hug him. She tried humoring him, but he was not to be humored. He continued to cry and sob, like a small child. Maya just stroked his head. It wasn't till morning that he finally became calm again. Even so, that night, he did make a promise to her, but one which, as far as she was concerned, was quite unnecessary.

"Listen to me, Maya," he said, "I haven't forgotten what I told you. I'm going to keep on trying and, if all goes well, by the end of next year, to usher in the New Year, I'll have saved up enough money to take you to Singapore."

But a year later Widi's luck still hadn't change. He almost couldn't bear it any longer. Maya had even been forced to sell some of her jewelry to pay for the children's school fees, which had made him feel even more worthless.

Widi felt like a hunted man. Set aside a little extra money? Heck, he was beginning to have trouble just keeping up with his regular job.

Widi's state of mind distressed Maya to no end. "There's no use fretting over nonsense, dear," she tried to tell him. "I'm not a greedy woman. You've given me wonderful children. You've taken care of me, and given me your love. I'm not going to demand now that we go to Singapore if it's beyond our means."

Maya's forbearance was not enough to assuage his feelings. It wasn't just that he wanted to take Maya on a trip abroad as he had promised; he needed also to satisfy himself. He needed to know that he was a person who could keep his promises. Perhaps more than anything else, it was this that most oppressed him: he had fallen short of his own expectations.

"It's like he's angry for not being as good as he had thought he was," Maya confided one day to a close friend.

In the end, Maya had been forced to leave him to his own torment, to let him be haunted by the desire to go abroad. It was for him, it seemed, a kind of mental hobby to keep him occupied in his old age.

"I know what she's thinking," Widi had said to his best friend, in reference to his wife's attitude. "I know she loves me, and she's as understanding a person as anyone could be, but she doesn't realize that it's not just myself I'm thinking of. I think she has the right to insist on getting what I promised her." He explained further, "If I do manage to take her abroad, it's not me who's supposed to be happy; it's her. If I'm the only one who's happy, that would defeat the whole purpose."

And so it was that every year, as New Year's approached, Widi found himself in the same state of fortune. The situation made him increasingly troubled, ever more despairing. Today, for instance, with New Year's on the horizon, he was visibly agitated. "Everyone calls it 'New Year's'," he grumbled, "but nothing in life is ever new. It's always the same routine, always the same old thing, over and over."

But this year it was a bit different from previous years when Widi had been more acquiescent: this time he would do something about it. And so he started buying lottery tickets again. He took on extra work. He tried to borrow money from a few of his friends. He even tried his hand at a little gambling. "Who knows?" he said. "Maybe that's where the key to success lies."

But all his efforts were for nought. They didn't so much add to the thickness of his wallet as much as they took a toll on his health.

Maya warned her husband to take care of himself. "If you get sick, it won't be just the trip to Singapore you jeopardize, but our weekly shopping money as well."

196

Widi listened, mute.

"And supposing you do scrape enough money to go abroad, don't forget we have the children to think of, too. Wouldn't it be better to put the money away in savings for them? What's the point in us going abroad now?"

"I made a promise," Widi sighed.

"Sure, you made a promise. But even way back then, if we had had the money to go abroad, we still would have thought, what's the point? And don't forget that if you're going to go abroad, it's not enough just to buy the ticket. You have to figure in the cost of meals and accommodations, too. And then money to buy presents to bring back, because if we went abroad, the relatives are going to straightway think that we have money to spare. If we were to come home empty-handed, we'd just make enemies. So, you see, going abroad is more likely to make you enemies than make you happy. So, enough already, forget about that crazy idea of yours."

But Widi was still Widi. He couldn't just shoo the idea from his mind. He thought things over, ruminated on Maya's admonition, but still came to the same conclusion. He still felt that he had to pick himself back up and find something that could change his life before New Year's.

"This is it," Widi said to his friend. "I'm going to try one more time to give Maya a New Year's gift that's really special. It's now or never. I'm not getting any younger, and by next year the children will be older and require more of our attention. Which means that this is the year I have to make good on my promise."

After he recovered from his bout of illness, Widi secretly renewed his efforts. He applied himself to the full but proceeded with caution, lest Maya learn what he was up to. She was to remain in the dark as to how or what or by which means, what strings he pulled, what opportunities he availed himself of, and what connections he used. He gave it all his best and, at last, there came a day when a smile appeared on the man's face.

When Widi came home that day, an envelope in his hand, his face shone. The gleam that had long since dimmed now reappeared. He was even singing softly as he entered the front door!

Maya was delighted by her husband's behavior, but she didn't say anything; she had a feeling that her husband had a surprise waiting for her. Out of the corner of her eye she noticed the calendar and her heart skipped a beat. Could Widi have succeeded in his plans for doing something special for the coming New Year?!

Neither one spoke much at the dinner table. Maya looked at Widi. There was still a smile on his face. She began to suspect that his smile might in fact be concealing something and began to grow more circumspect. Meanwhile, all Widi could do was grin with apparent glee.

"So what's up?" Maya finally inquired, after they had finished eating.

Widi smiled. "First make me some coffee."

Maya made him some coffee.

"So what is it?" she asked impatiently, pushing the coffee to him.

Widi laughed. "Guess!"

This time it was Maya who laughed nervously.

"I don't dare, I'm afraid I'll guess wrong. Just tell me. You're obviously pleased about something. Is there something good in store for us? What is it?"

Widi kept smiling.

"Tell me."

"Is it that you don't want to guess, or that you already know?"

"I don't know anything."

"Really?"

"Really."

Widi took a deep breath. He then extracted the envelope from his briefcase and put it down in front of Maya. It was a plain, but thick, envelope. Maya glanced at it but hesitated to pick it up.

"What's this?" she asked.

Widi nodded his head contentedly. "I'm not going to tell you because you can see for yourself what it is. Why don't you ask me how I got it?"

Maya smiled. "Okay, how did you get it.

Widi took another deep breath and closed his eyes before he began to speak. "After thirty years of trying, we've finally done it. I know you know how hard I've worked these past thirty years. We've hoped, we've done everything that we could, but luck has never been on our side. What we've gotten in return has never come close to how hard we've toiled. Maybe we're jinxed. Maybe we've been cursed. Who knows, but it's always seemed like something or someone has been keeping our ship from coming in.

"And I almost gave up. I hated life. I felt so ashamed that I came close to killing myself. I'm just lucky that you were always here, by my side. Luck is a scarce commodity..."

Widi talked for a long time. Maya listened to him, deeply moved. Now and then she bit her lip to ward off the threat of pain. Not infrequently she was forced to wipe away her sudden tears.

Widi, meanwhile, became more and more intent on calling up all their past sufferings until he, too, began to cry.

The couple cried and cried.

Finally Widi took Maya's hand in his, then placed the envelope in her hand.

"I managed to get these tickets for your New Year's present."

Maya's fingers, intertwined with her husband's, formed a circle, in the middle of which was the white envelope. Both were silent, still overcome by sadness or joy or, perhaps, despair. Widi was beyond words. He waited for Maya to speak.

"Thank you, dear," she finally said. "Listening to you just now has made me a very happy person. You will never know how much I appreciate all that you have done. You've worked so hard, you've made yourself sick. I appreciate that. That alone is enough of a New Year's present for me. Husbands like you, who after thirty years of marriage, still love and look after their wives the way you do are few and far between. That is worth much more than these tickets. That does me more good, makes me happier as a woman. Take these tickets and return them to the airline. Get your money back and put it away somewhere safe. Who knows, inflation might jump next year and give us more expenses to worry about. I swear to you before God that your hard work has just about broken my heart, but has brought me much happiness, too."

Maya pressed the envelope into her husband's hand. Widi tried to pull his hand away but the look Maya gave him was one of heartfelt love and assurance.

"You know what it is I'm trying to say, don't you? You're always able to understand me, aren't you?"

"Yes."

"Then you'll understand why I'm asking you to return the tickets. That's what will really make me happy. The fact that we can stop daydreaming, that you'll no longer be haunted by fantasies, that is more than enough for me as a New Year's present. You understand, don't you?"

Without waiting for an answer, Maya kissed her husband on the forehead and immediately hastened to clear away the table. Suddenly the situation was normal once more and Widi felt that there was no point in discussing the tickets further.

"Take a nap or read the paper, why don't you?" Maya suggested in a normal tone of voice as she took the leftovers to the kitchen. "I have to go over to the neighbor's to see their new baby."

Widi inhaled deeply. He stared at the envelope. The radiant look he had on his face when he came home was now one of severity. But after a while the severity lessened and he returned to normal. Normal that is, for other ordinary and uncomplicated husbands.

He rose slowly and, taking the envelope with him, went into the bedroom. He locked the door. In the privacy of the bedroom he opened the envelope and took out a thin sheaf of note paper. There were no tickets inside the envelope at all.

Widi didn't know if his wife was aware of his fabrication but he did know that, in the dining room earlier, something wonderful had transpired: He, a husband, had finally managed to make good his promise and Maya, his wife, had selflessly renounced his promise, for she placed a far greater value on her husband.

Widi sat on the bed, lost in thought. Tears welled in his eyes. Maya must have known. She really was an extraordinary person. "That is the best New Year's present I could ever hope for," he whispered.

At that same moment, in the kitchen doing the dishes, Maya also was crying. "Oh, dear Lord, have mercy. Please don't let him know that I know what was in the envelope," she murmured almost inaudibly. "We may be simple folk, but we have aspirations just like anyone else. We've suffered and we've put on this charade because that was the only way to keep on going and to find some happiness in the midst of poverty."

At the sound of the children's footsteps, some going towards the bedroom, others toward the kitchen, both Widi and Maya, simultaneously, wiped away their tears. They erased all tension from their features and put their smiles back on: their children, at least in their own minds, were not yet ready to have to taste such bitterness.

1982

TRANSLATED BY MARC BENAMOU

SENO GUMIRA AJIDARMA

The River's Song

DAWN WAS BREAKING beyond the forest. Still drowsy, I saw it from behind the awning of the boat whose motor roared like a hungry dragon. The journey still wasn't over. When had I left Tenggarong? The Kelinjau River twisted and turned amid the forest, its banks sometimes denuded and heaped with logs. For a day and a night I had lounged about in this boat. I thought we would soon arrive at Muara Ancalong. In my notebook I had written "a journey to examine my heart." My fantasies had evaporated, taken by the wind to wherever it would carry them. I thought of Jakarta, of the many-colored lights along the streets, of a hostess' bawdy laugh during a disco number at a bar.

A hornbill flapped its way across the river. At that very moment, Sureni, the steersman's wife, stuck her head out from behind the mosquito net.

"How far along are we?"

"We've passed Senyiur," her husband, Zaelani, answered while turning the tiller with his foot. A persistent mist hung over the river; the bank was dotted with bathers. I scooped a handful of the water flowing past the boat and wet my face. It wouldn't be too long before we arrived at Muara Ancalong, I thought. That meant that we would soon be parting ways, as the boat was bound for Wahau while I was heading for Tanjung Manis. The river forked after Ancalong, one branch to Wahau and one to Tanjung Manis.

The sun rose higher and the forest, which just awhile ago had been a dense black, became a cool shade of green. For millennia the forest had been unchanged. An otter peered shyly from the underbrush, while above, in a towering tree, proboscis monkeys turned their heads around like people in a daze. Sureni rose with a start and walked, hunched over, to the stern; the boat's cover was not high enough to allow a person to stand upright. Another head appeared beside the mosquito net, followed by yet another. I heard phrases of Kutai Malay, a language I could not understand well if spoken quickly. A baby cried. The two people quickly tidied their mosquito net and rolled up their mattress, thereby creating an open cabin and transforming the vessel back into a proper riverboat.

The boat's movement created waves that rippled towards the bank. I sat cross-legged on the side of the deck, trying to imagine what was within the forest beyond. Viewed from the river, it was difficult to get a sense of the destruction of the Kalimantan forest. The one or two timber camps we had passed gave a poor reflection of the grave destruction which had occurred. I knew for certain that the impression would be far different were I flying overhead in a plane chartered from Samarinda.

The journey seemed endless. The engine sputtered and Zaelani pulled the rope above his head four times – ting, ting, ting, ting! – as a sign for Bosu in the engine room to spur the engine to full speed ahead. As if to make up time and reassure me, the boat gathered speed. But Zaelani appeared to be uneasy, too. He looked at his wife and she stared back at him.

"What time will we get to Ancalong?" I asked.

"Maybe another hour and a half."

Several outboard-motor boats from the opposite direction zipped past. Maybe Ancalong was not too far after all. Along the river such boats were always found near settlements. I laid back. Whether quickly or slowly, we would arrive eventually. I closed my eyes, letting my thoughts fly to Masri and her incredible smile.

The boat was about twenty meters long, and perhaps some four meters wide. The two families on board I had met in Tenggarong. Apparently they were related. I was now the only passenger headed for Ancalong; the others weren't going far, only to the nearby settlements of Sebulu and Muara Kaman. Zaelani and Sureni appeared to be recently married, but Soda and Risa had two children, who were now fast asleep in cloth hammocks slung beneath the boat's cover. From their facial similarities I gathered that Soda was Sureni's elder brother. Sureni was forever busy in the cook-house. Yesterday, the boat had stopped long enough to buy fish from a seiner. The boat was its owners' sole source of income, taking on and dropping off passengers the length of the river. In the interior, the river was the artery of communication. But the boat was equally ready to become a floating home, especially so in the evening when the mosquito nets were hung, not only to ward off mosquitoes, but to serve as a family room. The netting was not the see-through kind, but was made from unbleached cotton, so closely woven that one could not see what went on inside it.

The sun rose higher but not a single house appeared, not even a notched-log ladder leading up from the water's edge to the top of the bank, indicating a village. I noticed that Sureni had replaced Zaelani at the tiller. Zaelani slept soundly as though nothing untoward could happen. The river current ran swifter the farther upstream one went. The forest became denser. We should have arrived at Muara Ancalong by now, I thought. But although I waited, it never appeared. I became uneasy, though the others seemed quite calm.

Sureni appeared from the stern. "Join us for food," she told me.

I said nothing but moved forward, stooping as I made my way past Risa, whose younger child was suckling at her breast. The older child rocked, asleep, in her lap.

205

Our meal was hard and crusty rice with a bit of fish, but I ate ravenously amid the roar of the engine.

I STARTED WITH SURPRISE, realizing that the sun was far to the west. Where were we? I hadn't fallen asleep and however slow the boat, we should have arrived by then. But there was Soda, sitting quietly. He couldn't have taken a wrong course. Wahau was just beyond Ancalong; there were no alternate routes.

I had to ask: "What's taking so long to get there?" But when Soda turned towards me, the look in his eyes was one I would never forget. His eyes, as if made of glass, were motionless, not even blinking, as if they had no soul. I dropped my gaze and looked around me. Everyone seemed to be in a daze, as if fatigued by an exhausting task.

Overhead, the sun sank closer to the horizon, but the sky's growing beauty heightened my sense of isolation. I felt more and more uneasy. The forest grew darker and more mysterious. The river's surface shimmered red in the evening sun. Soda still appeared transfixed and I tried to calm myself by thinking I must have misunderstood the journey's distance. I knew that this boat did not regularly make the trip downstream. Thus, these people were not fully conversant with the river's numerous bends. Perhaps my worry was just a feeling I had, mixed with a little fantasy. On a journey such as this a person can feel he is floating, suspended somewhere between joy and sadness, fear and courage, loneliness and curiosity.

The motor chugged as the boat traced the river's bends. Twilight was not all that red; it came in clumps of dark clouds, followed by drizzle and wind. The awning was lowered, but not before my trousers were wet from the sudden rain. The sky turned suddenly dark and Zaelani took over from Soda at the tiller, steering the boat confidently. The yellow light of reflective lanterns tried to penetrate the darkness. Outside it had become pitch black; I couldn't see even a meter ahead. Now and then submerged tree trunks scratched the boat's hull. The rain hissed down, heavier and heavier.

This new phase of the journey was one I had no choice but to follow through if I were to win my struggle with anxiety, this nightmare of shadows. Somewhere between sleep and watchfulness I heard a clear and soothing voice. Maybe it was just the sound of the water cleft by the prow of the boat, a song of constant rhythm, gentle and friendly. But sometimes there were other voices. Zaelani tried to wipe the glass of the window in front of the tiller. Now the night was misty outside and the boat's lanterns were turned toward the bank to help us maintain enough distance from the shore to keep us from running aground. I searched in my pockets for a *kretek*, my clove cigarettes, but they were gone. I remembered that in my backpack were some filter cigarettes given me on the plane. They tasted foul, but I searched for them anyway. I couldn't find them.

The wind howled and the infants began to cry. One, after Risa put him to her breast, immediately settled down, but the other child continued to cry while crawling here and there. I tried to sleep, and between the muffled sound of the engine and the murmur of voices, my dreams were indistinct: each time I awoke, I found myself still on the boat in a situation not much different from that in my dream.

Hours passed; I saw no sign of whatsoever of habitation. There were no logging company camps. There were no villages. There were no encounters with rafts of logs filling the river's course. And there were no more boats of the Dayak people with their elongated ear lobes. There was only the interminable forest, to the right and left of the river. In time the rain changed back to a drizzle. Ting, ting, the bell rang twice, a sign for Bosu to reduce speed and pump the water from the bilge.

If only you were here, I said to myself, thinking of Mastri and wondering if this journey would have filled her with happiness or fear. She was in Bali, quite possibly dancing for tourists in a big hotel at that very moment. And I was here. How could I suddenly find myself here, caught in darkness?

"An adventure is good only when you're talking about it," she insisted, "not when you're experiencing it." That indeed seemed to be the problem. An adventure is attractive only after it is over. And its attractiveness depends on the way the story is told, like a film you don't want to end, even after the final scene. But it does end, even as reality continues. And this would never end! I jumped up, remembering the glassy, soulless eyes of the others.

"You'll never make it to Wahau" I screamed. "Listen to me, you'll never reach Wahau! We should have arrived at Ancalong yesterday!" The others turned slowly towards me with cold looks. The drizzle had died and dull rays from the lanterns made their faces immobile, like totems. Even the two children seemed stiff. For a moment I thought they looked at me with pity, but their gaze implied they didn't care. They kept silent. I felt drained of strength and returned to the side of the boat, completely alone.

The engine continued to roar, as if all was in order. The wind blew, caressing my tense face. I was tense. Yes, I did think too much about myself. Maybe I wouldn't make it to Tanjung Manis, but that, in itself, was not important. What was the problem if I never arrived? Or if I never returned to Jakarta? To never return home. No, that was no longer important. Why did everything have to end with going home? What is home? What to do?

Mastri's performance was probably over. She would leave the hotel and return by van to Ubud. I couldn't stop thinking of her captivating smile, though not the one she wore when she was dancing. It was a pity she was married, though that was not really a problem. Anyway, I was married too.

Soda took over the tiller from Zaelani once more. Strange there was no question on their faces, as if it were not peculiar that we had not arrived at Ancalong. Sureni and Risa put up the mosquito net. I spread out the rush mat which they had lent me and lay down. Zaelani joined Sureni inside their tent. The air seemed extraordinarily cold. I wrapped my arms around my chest, hugging myself as tightly as possible.

Outside, the rain came again, heavily.

I DIDN'T NOW HOW LONG I SLEPT, yet, when I opened my eyes, the world was changed. I accepted that I really would not arrive in Ancalong. There was no need to question the matter further. My fellow passengers beamed with pleasure. Soda held the tiller in a relaxed and easy fashion. Sureni blinked happily. Slowly onward churned the boat, the sound of its engine a purr. The children appeared contented and calm.

The morning light shone beautifully. Zaelani was very happy. What had taken place? I was going to ask Risa but her attention was on her baby. She looked so Madonna-like, the scene so tender, I hesitated to disturb the mood. I felt I must be more resolute. Forest flanked the river's edge, the thick foliage gleaming silver, drenched by the morning light. Dewdrops fell, one by one, spiralling downward from the leaves and disappearing into the river.

No, we were not going anywhere. Certainly not upstream. This river had no headwaters. There was no upstream and no longer a downstream either.

Bosu's face shone so brightly. I would have no more terrifying nights. Our world would be like this forever, glowing constantly. This was no adventurer's tale. This was reality itself.

The river ran just as it had yesterday, just as it had since its creation. When Zaelani took over the tiller from Soda, I saw that their eyes held so much passion I wasn't sure of my own feelings. Zaelani pulled the rope four times – ting, ting, ting, ting! – and the boat surged forward on a sure course. Sureni tidied the mosquito net which had been taken down but was not yet folded.

1988

TRANSLATED BY E. EDWARDS MCKINNON

Holy Communion

IT WAS THREE O'CLOCK in the morning. Our Land Rover crawled in the dimness of the dying moon over the steep and winding road towards Prapat. The huge island in the middle of the lake looked like a reclining giant. Prapat sits on a promontory, her electric lights blending with the moonlight flickering off the restless waters – an ocean liner at anchor.

Emotion welled up within me – home! – but there was no joy or happiness.

By the Padang food stall, which was open round the clock, several large trucks loaded with rubber were waiting for their drivers and helpers who were inside eating plates of hot rice. The men's weather-bitten bodies were wrapped in heavy clothes. They were heading toward the Aceh-East Coast border, toward the harbors notorious as smuggling and bartering centers with Singapore and Penang. They were hauling rubber from the Pakan Baru area, a distance of a thousand kilometers to the south, not following economic rules exactly but, instead, the winding roads of the black market, black like the roads to the lake at night.

"A tire now costs forty thousand rupiah," someone remarked though no one had asked the question.

I wondered what the rental would be for a truckload and what they would be carrying on the return trip from the smuggling area.

My brother, who had been driving the borrowed Land Rover since Medan, was also a truck operator. While eating he talked about prices and ended up asking for a jerry can of gasoline from one of the drivers.

I knew that we still had some gas in reserve, but we had to go clear around the lake, across the whole southern area, to get to our village in the West. We would need as large a supply as possible. The rest of the road, especially so early in the morning, would be desolate – wide grasslands alternating with heavy forests – and there would be no place to buy gas.

All through the night, till the early morning when we were beyond Prapat, my brother had not said a single word. He concentrated on his driving, going at such a speed it was as if he was chasing after something. He had been driving that way since leaving Medan the day before.

It was not until around five in the morning that we encountered our first obstacle: a group of women pounding *pandan* leaves, the raw material for mats, on the roadbed. Then, at another spot along the road, a group of silent farmers on their way to their fields with farming tools in their hands forced us to slow down.

Even without an exchange of words, I knew the same picture occupied my brother's mind as it did mine: Father's face. Would I still see him alive? The same question haunted us. The doctor had estimated Father's age, based on his jawbone and teeth, at one-hundred thirteen years. The Old-Age Ceremony had already been held for him several times in the last few years. Each time Father had assumed that his death was near – yet he had kept on living.

But what was that to me? I didn't come for another ceremony but because my brother came to Jakarta specifically to fetch me. He said: "Father is suffering too much. He's run out of strength. It would be better if he rested forever. But that's not likely to happen till he sees you for the last time".

After my brother had finalized the purchase of a truck we left Jakarta for Sumatra.

Towards daybreak we reached the high plateau of wide open fields. The plain, which looked golden in the early sunlight, looked even brighter now because of the glittering morning dew.

Where are the herds of horses now? I asked myself. The neighing of horses, which symbolized the freedom of the plains and the strength of these mountains, became louder in my memories. We had traveled for tens of kilometers, yet we had not seen a single horse. Times had changed but the road was still not asphalted. It was only hardened with rocks.

Horses, the lake, the wilderness, hills soaring to the sky, sunburnt humans counting the passing ages by generations, measuring their suffering against their happiness in making sacrifices for their children and weighing their love by the viscidity of the mud in the rice field. Father was determined not to die until he had seen me.

We stopped at a village in the middle of a forest and I was introduced to the residents. Family! Blood relatives, descendants of the nth generation from the same ancestor. Welcome!

I gave a child a ball that I had actually bought for the children of my relatives in the village.

"Any news about Father?" my brother asked them.

"Nothing yet," several of them answered.

"But luckily *he's* here now," one of them remarked, with a glance in my direction.

We came across a lumber truck in the middle of the forest, but no one was around. My brother hit the horn of the Land Rover. From somewhere in the forest, axes resounded several times in acknowledgement. Ships in the mist calling out to each other, a melody carrying a message. We drove on without comment.

A little while later my brother said, "That was what's-his-name's truck! Father's alright," he then added.

213

"How do you know?" I asked.

"That truck wouldn't be up into the mountains if something were the matter with him," he answered. "The whole Western area and Samosir Island, too, are ready for Father's celebration."

He meant Father's death and the great funeral ceremony that would be held after.

"It will last four days and four nights," he said. "Seven days is too long for a celebration nowadays. Four days should be enough time for all the relatives from all over Batak Land to come to the party. A telephone-courier system has been set up so that when Father dies the news of his death can be spread quickly."

As we descended to the valley by the lake we saw some villagers carrying firewood and lumber.

"That is the shopkeeper who is in charge of building the temporary shelters," my brother commented. "It will be like a fair with thousands of people coming from all over."

"ALL SIX OF YOU are now here in front of me," Father said after the evening meal.

My youngest brother translated Father's words after reading the mumbling lips of his toothless mouth. Anything we had to say to Father had to be spoken into his ear slowly and loudly.

We sat cross-legged in a semicircle around him, we brothers awaiting Father's words.

"This is the first time that you are all together," he then said, referring to my presence. "I will present you with a feast. So find one of the buffaloes of our forefathers from the mountains!"

We brothers looked at one other in silence, muted not only by the solemnity of the message, but also by a practical question: how was one to capture a wild buffalo in the mountain wilderness, in the space of only one night?

Father was referring to the tens of wild buffaloes, remnants of the herd of hundreds our forefathers had bequeathed to him. The herd was a source of draught animals and of meat for feasts. But to capture one was difficult and usually took several days. First you had to search the jungle to find the herd, then you had to find the animal most suitable for the purpose.

Father made it clear that our ceremonial feast must take place the next day.

My eldest brother suggested allowing another day, but when this was passed on to Father, he answered curtly, "I said tomorrow."

Father then asked to be put to bed. He was tired.

The next morning Father smoked the cigar I had brought for him and he drank the milk sent by a relative from Jakarta. On that day, like on any other day, people came from near and far to see him. Some brought an offering of food for Father, to reciprocate for blessings received, just as if Father were a holy man. Father signaled his acceptance of the offerings with a touch of his hand, but he ate nothing. When babies were placed in his lap to be blessed, he caressed their heads and smiled happily.

He requested a boiled egg from one old woman. A bottle of sulfur water from somebody else. Limes to make his bath water fragrant from yet another person. Everybody set out to fulfill his requests. They ran home to their villages, happy that they were able to fulfill Father's final requests. It was only later that I realized that their happiness was due to Father's generosity. Father knew that the villagers were poor and he made it possible for them to ask for his blessings by requesting things that were still within their ability to give. He did not ask for expensive rituals.

Later that afternoon we heard cheering on the mountain slope, echoing with the sound of the Land Rover. The men had managed to find and shoot a young buffalo cow, just as Father had requested, for the offering in the sacred meal he wished to share with us, his children.

The leader of the hunt proudly reported his success to Father.

From his resting place Father cut in, "Who said that my wishes will not be fulfilled? It is you people who have no faith." Then he went to sleep.

Father was awakened that evening after the ceremonial food was ready. It consisted of all the parts of the head, chopped up and cooked together in blood: tongue, ears, brains, meat, skin, bones and the eyes. The liver was cooked whole.

My brother's daughter, the one who usually took care of him, roused him. "Grandpa, the food is ready." He was helped up from his bed and placed on the floor, leaning against the wall with a pillow in his back. "Are you all here?", he asked while moving his hand from left to right as if inspecting us.

"Yes, Father," said my eldest brother, already a grandfather himself.

"Where is the liver?" Father asked. One of his grandchildren pushed the plate with the steaming liver toward him. Father's favorite sharp knife was also on the plate.

"Now divide this liver into six parts," he ordered while touching the hot meat. His grandson cut the buffalo liver.

"Done, Grandpa," the grandson said. Father reached for the plate and took a piece.

"Come here," he said to us. My eldest brother came forward, then the second, the third, until finally it was my turn as the fifth son, to receive a piece of the liver of the sacrificial meat.

After waiting for each of us to finish eating our share, Father said: "You have eaten my gift of food. The six of you are my blood. And to you I command..." He paused like a minister at a religious ceremony. "To you I command what was taught by my forefathers to my grandfather, by my grandfather to my father, and by my father to me: to love one other, especially you as brothers, to help one other and to aid one other; to be united, to share your burdens...

"Remember that there are times when one who is younger or

poorer might be a better leader than you. Follow him! This is my message to you." Then he signalled that he wished to lie down again.

All present were moved by Father's words and fell silent. The local minister, who was also present, commented, "Just like in the Bible." The look on the pastor's face was one of obvious relief. He must have concluded that there had been no superstitious elements in the ceremony, something he had previously feared.

The meal proceeded cheerfully, livened up by conversation and bursts of laughter. There was happiness, harmony, and peace. In the evening Father asked for *hasapi* players to play his favorite melodies. But when they began to play traditional songs with a modern beat, Father got angry. He asked for help to get up and go to bed. With guilty looks on their faces, the musicians shifted to playing the tunes in the traditional way. Father nodded happily as he listened to the sound of the lutes. But after a while he suddenly commanded the players to stop. He lifted his face as if he were going to pronounce another message. And, he did: "Tomorrow... I want to offer a prayer to the god of Pusuk Buhit!"

Everybody was startled. The prayer to the god of Pusuk Buhit, the quintessence of Batak pagan rituals, was condemned by Christian law! Imagine, paying homage to the gods of the Holy Mountain! "Call the *gondang* players from Limbong," he said. He asked for the most famous ceremonial drum player by name, supposedly the only musician in the region still capable of correctly playing the music for the ceremony of homage to Pusuk Buhit.

Like all of Father's requests or messages, this one, too, was a command shrouded with magic overtones to people around him. And although it was difficult to ignore religious considerations, the command was nonetheless obeyed.

That night father called for me specifically to come and sit by his resting place. He had a message for me: "The day after tomorrow you will return. Go. I know you have lots of work."

The next night, after the *gondang* players arrived, preparations were made for the Pusuk Buhit ceremony. A number of people, at the behest of the pastor, had tried to dissuade Father but to no avail.

The ceremony – which I myself had never seen before and had only heard about – was very solemn and at the same time, like all pagan rituals, frightening. Though Father himself did not eat pork, the sacrifice for the ceremony was a pig, dressed and cooked in a special way as befitting an offering to the gods.

During the ceremony all fires and lights in the village were to be extinguished. No one was allowed to cross the grounds or to go in and out of the houses. All doors and windows had to be tightly closed.

The villagers knew about the ritual and, by evening, no one dared to leave his house.

At exactly seven o'clock, the *gondang* sounded. The darkness seemed to emphasize the eerie, mystical quality of the music. Inside the house, Father, outfitted in full traditional dress, was helped to stand and lift the platter containing the sacrificial pig. He was now ready for his mystical devotion: to meet and be united with the spirits of his forefathers, creatures far beyond the reach of earthly eyes, beyond words, even feelings, on top of Pusuk Buhit.

THE NEXT MORNING I took leave from father who was lying on his sleeping place. It seemed as if Father had become a stranger to me since the previous night but, at the same time, he seemed quite close. When I took my leave I whispered in his ear, "Father, I am leaving!" He nodded and dozed off again.

I started my journey home by taking the shortcut across the lake. Arrangements had been made for the boat to pick me up in the cove of the valley of the village where I was born. The boat trip would end in Prapat, a stop for busses bound for Medan.

When the boat reached the middle of the bay I looked back towards the village, which was still asleep in the haziness of the early morning.

To the right Pusuk Buhit soared clearly into the grayish blue sky. As I lit a cigarette to ward off the cold wind, it struck me that for all my adult life Father had never talked to me except for that night when he sent me off. "Go," he had said. "I know that you have lots of work!"

1964

TRANSLATED BY TOENGGOEL P. SIAGIAN

SITOR SITUMORANG

Jinn

I.

AT DAWN THE SKY becomes incumbent with the dazzle of sunlight reflecting off the crystal lake. The sun, the color of pastel silk, warms the morning sky. The air is kinetic with the hush of a thousand whispering voices.

The wind's breath does not touch the edge of the lake, yet grasses sway for below a snake slithers. Bees buzz. The stillness of the scene is made animate by the flapping of dragonfly wings. The firmament trembles silently.

AMAN DOANG LAY stretched out upon the matted grass, staring upwards, unseeing, at the blue sky. He mused but was himself unaware of his own thoughts. Nature's blanket lay over him and he, silent and unmoving, lay beneath, as if waiting for something to break the silence.

Aman Doang stood, then walked towards the water's edge. There, while washing his face, he was for a moment transfixed by the mirror image of his own face resting on top of the water. Beneath the diaphanous vision fish glided slowly through the water.

Aman Doang raised his head to look across the bay, and then farther beyond, across the lake's expanse. His eyes rested on the bald mountain peering from the water a few hundred meters away. Laughter from young women cutting grass for thatch on the mountainside floated through the air and towards him like ripples on the water. Aman Doang turned to look behind him. Terraced fields of rice made ladders descending to the nest of villages lying in the gorge below.

The road back to Aman Doang's village from the lake passes by the graveyard and there, at the cemetery, Aman Doang stopped to stare momentarily. A herald of fitful screams rushed through the sky and bounced off the vale's embankment to fall on the neck of the mountain that pinched the bay. Faint and mournful, the whispered cries slipped down the slope and slid into the water to precipitate to the lake's bottom. And strangled, there they lay, in the kingdom of Boru Saniang Naga, the lake's goddess. Far below, on the lake's bed, is her earthly residence, a place where no human can safely go to and return from, a place where the victims of the storms that rage atop the lake in the dry season reside. The wind, racing down the mountainside like a behemoth boulder, smashes into the water, stirs it, churns it, throws up into the air waves as high as rooftops. And into the whirling water the sleek fishing boats are drawn. Sucked beneath the surface, they are pulled into the world below, not ever to return. Although the villagers search for the victims, the victims never return. Riding the waves in their crafts the villagers strike gongs, hoping the storm's victims will find their way back to the human world. But Boru Saniang Naga releases only the victims' bodies. Corpses rise to the water's surface, but souls remain behind, securely shackled and bound, as reparation for human sin.

The water goddess is beautiful! But she is cruel.

So it was that the soul of Saulina, Aman Doang's younger sister, was not freed. For a day and a night the gongs sounded before her corpse was found. But her soul had already been taken from her.

Aman Doang's young son crawled on the ground beside him, playing on the bare ground as he himself sat repairing his hoe. And then, that weird and eery cry... How could he have known that his own sister was in danger? How could he have known that the village head was even then spending his lust on the honor of a young woman, his sister, Saulina? And while he and the other people of the village sat peaceably unaware, Saulina, his sister, threw herself into the lake.

Boru Saniang Naga returned only her corpse. The village head was discharged from his post and sentenced to three months in jail. Other than that, what more could be done? Aman Doang's family was only one among many and survival of the community depends on majority support.

Aman Doang walked stiffly homeward. A number of villagers lolled beside the entrance to the village. Aman Doang veered from the path and passed through the brush and bamboo grove lining the top of the bulwark to enter his home from the back. Such shame he felt. It would be that way forever now.

Entering the dimly lit central room of the house, Aman Doang glanced at his father. The old man looked at his son. Their eyes met but the old man made no attempt to greet him. Aman Doang looked upwards. Thin shafts of moonlight entering the house through holes in its thatch roof pierced the darkness that hung above them.

That night, after the day's final meal, the household retired. Aman Doang stole out of the house and crept out of the village towards the rice fields.

"I'm going to open the water gate to the field...."

No one heard his muttered statement; Aman Doang was the only one not yet asleep. His father coughed intermittently but he, too, was sound asleep. Before leaving the house Aman Doang had pulled a knife from a crack between the wall boards which he now sharpened on a river stone. The moon appeared. Clouds washed over the crystal sphere but passed by to permit it to shine brightly again. Blackened mountains loomed around him. Moonlight shone upon him. Inside the village bulwark, buffaloes lowed. Aman Doang walked back to the village. The ground beneath his feet had taken on the pale shade of the silvery gray moonlight that swaddled the village. The light crept beneath the houses where villagers stabled their animals. Six head of buffalo rested beneath the house of the village head.

Startled by Aman Doang, the buffalo became restless, knocking their horns against the pillars that supported the house. "Who's out there?" a voice called from above, inside the house. Aman Doang said nothing. His eyes were trained on the underside of the floorboards. A flash of yellow light – a kerosene lamp was lit – suddenly leapt through the loosely jointed slats. The light moved across the room and towards the door. Aman Doang saw first the village head's feet and then his sarong as the man cautiously descended the stairs. At the bottom of the steps the man stopped and stood still. He tilted his head slightly to the side as if listening for something. The bamboo, blown by the wind, swayed back and forth and the poles, rubbing against one other, released an eery refrain. Aman Doang stepped forward to attack. The man fell quickly, and lifelessly, to the ground. He had not even screamed. Aman Doang stooped to retrieve his knife, then left. Back at home, Aman Doang slept soundly beside his father.

In the morning the village head was found face down in the dusty ground outside his home. Next to his body was an overturned kerosene lamp. Cold, the lamp had apparently extinguished itself some time before. When Aman Doang entered into the circle of people that surrounded the corpse the huddle fell silent. Each member of the circle stared at the corpse and then tried to stop from staring at Aman Doang. Aman Doang's father had also learned of the death of the village head but did not join the onlookers. Not saying a word to anyone, the old man left the village, his lips moving silently but furiously, and hastened away in the direction of the lake.

Aman Doang said nothing, just as he said nothing throughout the course of his trial. Even when the final verdict was read out to him, he did not attempt a word of reproof. "Twenty years in prison!" Aman Doang was to be sent to Nusakambangan, the island prison on Java's south coast.

On the day the police took Aman Doang away, he was accompanied by his relatives to the lake's southern shore, the point from where he would depart for Java. Before boarding the police launch Aman Doang, his hands still shackled, was permitted to shake the hands of family and friends. Those who were there that morning said they saw in Aman Doang's eyes an incredible and weird light burning and that when he embraced his mother he gazed not at her, nor at anyone else there, but off and into the distance towards some unascertainable point in the heavens beyond the mountain peak. His gaze was no longer human, the people said, but that of a jinn, a spirit which had come to inhabit the man's physical body. And they also said that when shaking Aman Doang's hands they had felt not the warm clasp of a living man but the frigid clutch of a corpse.

No one ever returns from Nusakambangan.

On the day of Aman Doang's departure his father did not accompany him to the shore, and all during the trial his father had visited him only once. And even then he had done little but hold his son's hand. "Eat something, you have to eat," the old man prodded, as if he were a young child to be coddled. Aman Doang's mother dished out for him some rice she had cooked at home. But her son had no desire to eat.

For Aman Doang everything smelled of rotting corpses. For him, morning and evening had lost distinction. The sun no longer climbed in the sky and made its way across the heavens; it rested, fixed in one position on the horizon. And the moon hung suspended over the sky's center. Aman Doang's eyes carried the dull cast of the eyes of a dead fish. For him only the nights passed quickly. After being escorted back to his cell in the evening, the door was slammed shut behind him, and then suddenly it would be morning again. Though the chains he wore were heavy, their weight did not drag him down. His steps felt light. He was able to float on the water. And there was someone singing to him, calling out to him. It was Boru Saniang Naga.

The face of that woman... Who was she? Could that be his wife? No, no, it was a jinn, a spirit, and she was clutching a dead baby in her arms!

Thousands of fingers stretched out towards him and he fell helplessly backwards, rolling and tumbling downwards into a deep gorge. His fall was swift and, like a hardened clot of earth loosened from its mountainside cleft, there was no way to check his descent down its sheer side. Farther down he fell. Deeper and deeper. A chorus of moaning voices. Church bells began to ring. Clang! Clang! Clang! Three times they rang, a sign of death.

The engine of the launch came to life and the police led Aman Doang into the boat's small hold. Women keened but his father was not there among them — "I've put that knife there for you," his father had said. "I pray that God watches over you." — and then their voices died.

Soon the boat was but a small dot atop a shimmering blue expanse.

No one ever returns from Nusakambangan.

Only the village elders could say for sure how long Aman Doang was kept in prison. But long before his return to the village his wife had learmed to laugh again, though even when she laughed her face remained immobile and evinced no joy.

II.

SO AFTER FIFTEEN YEARS in the Nusakambangan Prison, Aman Doang returned home. On the birthday of the Dutch Queen an amnesty was declared and Aman Doang's prison term was reduced by five years. During the fifteen years Aman Doang had spent in prison not once had he sent a letter to his family. Not once had he received a letter from them. What was there to say? Aman Doang was dead. He had accepted that. Only when his mother had died and then later his father, had he been informed of any news from outside the prison.

By the time Aman Doang returned to his village, his wife had remarried, his son was sixteen years old. Aman Doang was dead.

Aman Doang had intended to work as a barber upon his return, as this was a trade he had learned in prison. But who would trust their head to the scissors of an ex-convict? Rumors spread that Aman Doang had been sadistically cruel in prison, that he was insane, and that it was because of his very wickedness that his sentence had been commuted and he had been granted an early release.

Then the story spread that in the night a gigantic serpent had visited the gorge. No one had witnessed the event, but there were those who had heard it, and the commotion the gigantic serpent created that night sounded like the thunder of a mountain falling through the air and smashing into the lake.

New life was also given to the old tale of the two shepherds, a brother and a sister, who, because of their love for each other, had been punished by the gods: Incest is not permissible. Just at the moment when the two embraced they had been turned to stone. Whenever Aman Doang passed by, people turned away to avoid his gaze.

Aman Doang disappeared from the village for a time. When he came back, he returned by boat from across the lake, carrying with him fishing supplies. After that he was rarely seen. He spent his days on the water, near the far side of the lake, far from human habitation. It was there he plied his boat and snared his fish.

The lake's rocky shore is infested with caves where fishermen will take a daytime nap and at night, shelter. But after Aman Doang's return the other fishermen stopped frequenting the caves. They said that Aman Doang now lived in the largest of the caves, a huge and gaping mouth in a giant slab of stone standing upright on the lake's far shore. From its centrum on the shore the stone slab soars into the air while its base thrusts itself deep into the water. The stone's base is buried so deep in the water that even on the clearest of days, when the surface of the water is completely motionless, it cannot be seen. It is near this slab that the largest fish in the lake are found but because the slab is considered sacred no fisherman is brave enough to try his luck there. When the fishermen pass that place all excess motion in their boats comes to a sudden halt. They take great care not to be too vigorous, dipping their oars slowly into the water and pulling them gently sternward so as not to break the water's surface nor raise ripples in the water. Ever so slowly the oars slice through the water. One would not want to disturb the gods.

The years passed and Aman Doang continued to live his life alone in that cave. It was said he married Boru Saniang Naga, the water goddess, and that each day she provided him his food, permitting him to catch the fish that made their home in the water around the sacred slab.

Each night for several years a flame, like a miniature torch, was visible, resting atop the black water of the lake's far edge. Then, one night, the flame did not appear. Unbroken blackness rimmed the lake's edge.

With each passing day the people of the gorge grew more nervous and frightened. There were those who said the gods were angry and that a sacrifice must be offered to them as propitiation for the souls of Aman Doang and his sister, Saulina.

The boats set off in a queue across the water while the inhabitants of the gorge, both old and young, beat their metal gongs. Blazing torches crackled beneath an ebony sky. The villagers paddled their way toward Aman Doang's cave. The gongs beat nonstop. A shaman stood at the prow of the lead boat to chase away the jinn who lined the watery road to Aman Doang's cave. Arriving at the slab, the people found the cave completely bare, save for the presence of a faded sarong, a cold hearth, and a heap of fish bones.

"Boru Saniang Naga has taken him!" The shaman recited a mantra and sprinkled the cave with citrus juice. A white chicken was ceremoniously killed.

THAT NIGHT, they say, the jinn fled from the cave and the souls of Aman Doang and his sister Saulina were calmed. Upon the order of Boru Saniang Naga, they then became the rightful inhabitants of the sacred stone. Since that time no one has thrown themselves into the lake. No one has been drawn into the water's depth. The gongs are silent now.

1955

TRANSLATED BY JOHN H. MCGLYNN

The Charm

MORE AND MORE PEOPLE came to the house with the glass windows. Muri, its owner, had just returned from his latest buying trip to the capital and it was getting time for him to distribute the gifts and souvenirs that he'd brought back for the assembly of friends and relations who had collected in his living room. But Muri's wife wasn't home. In fact she hadn't been home since morning, when she'd gone off to trade at the market.

Those who were expecting gifts waited patiently as Muri held forth on the many changes he had noticed in the capital since his last visit there five years ago, things that other people knew of only by way of the television screen. Most everyone in the village shared the hope of seeing for themselves what life in distant Jakarta was really like, but for most people this notion remained a distant dream. Only Muri, who was by far the richest man in the village, had ever gotten a chance to see the tall buildings that lined the streets of that great city.

Ismiyati, Muri's wife, was different from the rest. Even though her husband had begged her a thousand times over to go with him, she had no desire to see the big city. For Ismiyati, Muri's absence meant that she was free to visit Dullah, her "unofficial" spouse, who lived in the village across the river.

For Ismiyati, the village that Dullah lived in was one of unsurpassed beauty, though in fact it differed very little from her own. The same river flowed past both villages. Each village had its market in a large wooden shed with a roof of corrugated tin, and in both villages the market stood next to a broad field where the villagers played soccer and other ball games. The mosque in Dullah's village was the same, too – not much more than a house with an onion-shaped dome of sheet metal, no bigger no smaller than the dome of the mosque in Ismiyati's village. But in Dullah's village Ismiyati felt a special sense of calm. Her laughter came more easily there and she seemed to find much greater pleasure in life just from being able to be close to her lover as he plied his trade in the barber's stall outside the village's market.

Everyone knew that Ismiyati had taken Dullah as her lover, but no one had the nerve to tell Muri. They feared that he might bar them from working in his ricefields, which stretched along the main road outside the village. Then, too, they had also to think about Muri's jasmine gardens, located beyond the fields, away from the road. There one could always earn extra cash by gathering the blossoms and taking them to the market where they were used to make tea, or were made into the floral hairpieces which nowadays were considered an essential part of a bride's outfit. For a bride not to wear jasmine was to say that she was no longer a virgin. Professional bridal outfitters came from far and wide to Muri's house for his all-important jasmine flowers. Muri, in fact, was the local broker for virtually every commodity the village produced.

Dullah was not a young bachelor, but a middle-aged man who was famous for his sharp tongue. He was dark with skin the color of a mangosteen peel, and when he laughed he sounded like a hungry monkey. His only source of income was the little stall where he shaved and cut the hair of visitors to the village market. Muri, too, had once been one of his customers, but that was before Dullah had begun his affair with Ismiyati. Despite that, there wasn't any bad blood between the two men, as each had learned to keep his distance from the other – even as they both tried to win Ismiyati's heart, hoping each day it would be his turn to sleep with her.

So it was that when Muri went away, life in the village across the river became for Dullah and Ismiyati a celebration of love. When Muri was home they were able to meet only in the afternoons, but when he was out of town Dullah could hold Ismiyati in his arms through the night and into the early hours of dawn. Though of course the other villagers knew of the affair, no one dared reprimand the couple, not even the village chief. The chief was reminded of his unwritten duty whenever it became obvious that Ismiyati was spending the night with Dullah, but still he did nothing about it, remembering only too well the time Dullah had threatened to split open the skull of his wife if ever she stuck her nose in his business again. Dullah's threat thus effectively sealed the chief's mouth and made him put aside any intention he might have had of finding a way for Muri and Ismiyati to mend their fences. As a result the affair continued, with both Dullah and Muri competing for the love of the single woman whose beauty was the equal of any big-city prima dona.

As for managing time, it was Ismiyati who decided "when" and "with whom." No doubt she was an expert in channeling the two men's emotions, for Muri had never been given cause to lose his temper with his wife for not being there when he demanded his rights as a husband. The undeniable truth was that every time he needed Ismiyati, she was there – that is, of course, unless she'd gone to market. And wasn't that a legitimate reason for her absence, having to sell the lengths of batik cloth that her husband brought back from his trips to Central Java? No, every time Muri needed her, she was there, serving his coffee just the way he liked it – thick and just a little sweet – with a flirtatiousness that never failed to convince him that her heart had not been stolen by Dullah.

Dullah was in fact a kindhearted man, but because he had stolen part of his wife's affection, Muri had taken to calling him a thief.

Ismiyati merely smiled at her husband when he revealed his dislike of Dullah. "Why do you say such awful things about him?" she asked, coming to Dullah's defense. "He's just a barber, after all."

"Because he's turned your head!" Muri answered.

"Well, if he has," she responded, "then what am I doing still here with you?"

"But there's no telling what goes on in a woman's heart."

Ismiyati smiled. "Oh, please.... Everyone knows you're better looking than Dullah. What are you so worried about?"

"When you're crazy about someone, good looks don't even come into the question. So if you are crazy about him, what can I do about it?"

"Well, you're assuming a whole lot, that's all I have to say," Ismiyati told him. "Look at me. Here I am, right by your side. We make love every night... What more do you want?"

"Maybe we do, but I know that whenever you come home late it's because you've been with Dullah."

"Oh, is it?" she queried. "And I suppose you don't ever notice other girls. I know that there are lots of young and untried girls you could have any time you wanted."

"Who wants 'untried'? They don't know how to do anything."

"What do you mean, 'don't know how to do anything?'"

"Well, you know...." Muri paused. "Like what you do when I'm feeling in the mood."

When their conversation took a turn in that direction, Muri and Ismiyati usually fell into each other's arms, the one leading the other to new heights of pleasure, until it became evident that the bedroom was a better place than the dining room for what was to follow.

Muri never tried to check up on Ismiyati at Dullah's barber stall. He was afraid that Dullah, a man he viewed as belonging to a lower social stratum, might do something to embarrass him. Thus, if it happened that Ismiyati was late in coming home he would wait for her at the inlet next to the rice fields where the boat that carried Ismiyati home would dock. As soon as she came into view he would wade out to meet her and take her purchases into his arms so she wouldn't have to carry the burden home.

Muri was often struck by a deep-seated urge to ask her what had happened at the market that day, but he never voiced his question for fear that her response might not be the one he wanted to hear. Why should he stick the point of the knife into his own heart? His curiosity was thus never satisfied and he was always left with a vague suspicion of his wife's actions. Nonetheless, he always gave thanks that once again she had returned to their village. He knew that later that night they would laugh together, and that she would be ready and eager to please. So it was pointless for him to make accusations about what may or may not have happened over there in the market across the river. How could she, anyway?

THAT NIGHT, AS ON OTHER NIGHTS, their conversation was embellished with Ismiyati's coy remarks and Murni's doubting questions. When he asked her if her smiles and what seemed to him her unfeigned affection were honest or just a remnant of the attention she had given to Dullah earlier that day, he only half-accepted Ismiyati's supple embrace as an answer.

For Muri it seemed that the lovemaking that followed was less fulfilling and no longer the merging of two souls as it usually was.

The thought distressed him. "Do you still love me?" he asked her.

"Why are you asking that?"

"You're not Dullah's mistress, are you?"

"You're much better than Dullah."

"You always compare me to Dullah. You know very well who Dullah is, and who I am. Do you act this way with Dullah, too?"

"Dullah is just a friend," Ismiyati said. "You know he's not as close to me as you are."

Muri couldn't continue this line of questioning with its undertone

235

of accusation but in his heart he remained unconvinced that Ismiyati was his alone. And though he might not have the control over her that he wanted, it never crossed his mind to divorce his wife.

Why was it that when they were in bed together there was always something that marred his longing for her? Why was it, he asked himself that her embraces always left him with a vague feeling of emptiness?

He gazed intently at Ismiyati, sitting close to him on the edge of the bed rolling her waist-sash, then loosening her chignon so that her long hair fell free to her waist. She was a beautiful woman to look at, he silently confessed. What man in his right mind would divorce such a woman? Even as he asked this question he nonetheless felt a kind of paralysis arrest him. Who was it who really possessed that smooth and flawless body.

Muri didn't feel the slightest shred of anger or hatred towards his wife. Why then did he feel such a driving need to dominate her? This urge was like a cold night breeze, one fanning the fire of his maleness, setting alight in him a compulsion to be angry with the woman he had struggled so hard to win in marriage – but who now no longer seemed to belong to him at all. Of course he realized that God was the real owner of human life and that no person can really own another; even so he wanted to be seen as the one who possessed that wild and beautiful creature he had taken to be his wife. Where was the courage and manliness that once had made him the idol of every woman in the village? Where had they disappeared to?

In the old days it had been his name, and his name alone, on the lips of every eligible woman in the village. His name had passed frequently in the conversations that took place among women in the rice fields and at important social events. He had been famous for his ability to win out over all competition. It was a strength that he had prided himself upon.

He remembered the time when he had come to pay a call on

Ismiyati and had caught sight of Marjo, the chicken seller, running from her place, head over heels. That had been before they were engaged and there was any mention of a possible engagement! Even then other men had felt guilty when spending too much time with Ismiyati. He recalled the batik merchant *cum* rice broker who traded his goods in the village. He had been a man ever solicitous of Ismiyati, offering her batiks of the finest quality and pattern. But she had always refused his gifts with a gentle word or gesture and when he left her house, it was with a look of consternation and surprise, especially if he happened to find Muri waiting out front.

Where had the good name and the charisma that he'd always depended on in the past disappeared to? When he turned to Ismiyati with the intention of unloading his feelings, he found himself struck dumb by her gaze.

Could it be true that Ismiyati used some kind of charm – a *susuk*, perhaps? He had heard stories of the power of *susuk*, the tiny pins that shamans implanted under people's skin to magically enhance their attraction. How else could he explain his wife's mysterious power to bewitch every male who came into her presence? He knew of the rumor around the village: that even as a girl Ismiyati had acquired the power of meditation, that she had studied mystic arts with such-and-such a guru, and that she had had a *susuk* of precious stone inserted between her eyebrows. Whereas before that time she had been nothing special to look at.

Muri looked closely at his wife's face but could see no trace of a *susuk* between her eyebrows. Why did people say such things? He, as her husband, would surely know if she had one, wouldn't he?

Ismiyati smiled in her sleep, and Muri cradled her in his arms like a mother cradling a child. He looked closely at the skin between her eyes but saw no sign of perforation, nor the glow of any precious stone or metal. How could anyone, even a shaman or *dukun*, insert a charm there? It would hurt, wouldn't it? He wanted to ask Ismiyati and he shook her slightly to wake her up, but she only stretched and tightened her arms around his neck. He wanted to tell her to be truthful with him, to tell him whether it was true what people said, that a *dukun* had inserted a charm between her eyebrows. But tonight, as on many nights before, his questions remained unspoken and he found himself waiting for the sleep that he knew would not come until daybreak was close at hand.

If it weren't for that man Dullah, his life with Ismiyati would be perfect, Muri thought. He saw himself walking Ismiyati to the river that morning, carrying her wares to the spot where the ferryman docked his boat. Even then Dullah had no doubt been waiting on the other side of the river for Ismiyati's arrival. The same boat that took Ismiyati away from him carried her to that accursed market across the river.

Only after she had disappeared from view, swallowed by the fence of bamboo that lined the other shore, had Muri hurried away to take care of his daily chores: collecting payments from villagers who owed money on their debts to him and lending money to others who were in need.

He then thought of all the gifts he had brought home from the city just the day before. All remained untouched, even after Ismiyati had come home late that night.

By midday he had finished his collections and had gone home. He himself had unpacked all the goods he had worked so hard to accumulate on his trip to the city. First he'd taken out the green *kebaya* of Buginese silk fringed with lace – Ordinarily only the wife of the village chief ever wore such a blouse – and then the new hairpiece that Ismiyati had asked for. Following that, the slippers decorated with red coral beads which he knew would be a perfect final touch for Ismiyati's formal *kain* and *kebaya*. He knew that Ismiyati, dressed in these clothes, would be more than equal to the wife of the major he had seen in Jakarta.

The more gifts he had removed from his bags, the angrier he had felt towards Ismiyati. How could she have paid no attention to these gifts which he had bought with his hard-earned cash?

What he found especially galling was that she had come home so late that his own friends and relatives had been deprived of receiving their share of gifts and, one by one, they had returned home, disappointed and empty-handed. To make matters worse, he hadn't found the opportunity to apologize to them. But the strangest thing of all was that when Ismiyati had arrived home, he hadn't been able to get angry with her at all. So exhausted was she that all she had been able to do was drop her wares in a heap on the floor and fall asleep in his arms without even taking a bath first. She hadn't so much as tasted the bread, cheese and apples that he'd bought, luxury items that, as far as he knew, had never before been seen in the village. Year in and year out, the village produced the same things: bananas, soybeans, spinach, cassava, rice, jasmine flowers for tea, and sometimes mangoes, pineapples, and melons.

Muri went to the kitchen. He was seething inside but managed to calm himself and to dispel the loneliness of the quiet house by humming a tune. The silent house, with its glass windows – a rarity in this village – was his frequent companion when Ismiyati was away, having gone off to sell her wares. Is that what she was doing, selling her wares? What was it that she was selling? Herself? No, that couldn't be... They weren't lacking for money. He had no need for more wealth. He supposed that Ismiyati needed companionship, a friend to be with when the two of them were apart. Of course. It was then, during the long afternoon hours at the market when customers were few, that Dullah had drawn her to him, using the free time to joke and laugh with her, to attract her to him with his banter, his humor, and his willingness to laugh at the anecdotes she told him with a coquettish smile.

Damn! The thought of the two of them together made him so angry. He went into the kitchen, took out the machete he kept there, and then proceeded to the mango tree out behind the house where he sat down and began to sharpen the knife's blade. He continued to hum the tune that had kept him company earlier. As he worked the blade grew sharper and by early evening the machete was so sharp that when he tested the blade he was able to fell a young banana tree with a single blow. Chickens scratching near the tree fled to their pens with no need of encouragement from Muri's old maidservant, who had just come out of the house.

"What are you sharpening your machete for?" she asked Muri.

"To cut the throat of a beautiful woman."

"What woman?"

"Your boss!"

"Hush! You shouldn't even say such things. People might hear you."

Muri laughed loudly at this.

"I mean it. You could find yourself at the wrong end of a manhunt."

"So what?" Muri replied. "Life in prison might not be so bad. At least there you have lots of company. It's never lonely like it is here at home. And you don't have to think about making money."

"So who's forcing you to make money? You don't need money to be happy – as long as you have enough, that is. You don't have any children, so what's the fuss? You can't take it with you. The only things that count in the afterlife are good works and piety. You must be getting senile, saying crazy things like that."

"What do you mean, 'crazy'?"

"What you're saying is crazy. It's the talk of a madman. What happened to you in Jakarta? Did someone put a spell on you or something? You come home and start talking about murdering your wife – the very same woman you've shared your bed with for so many years and who has taken care of your every need. You've never given her any kids, but has she left you? Answer me that. How can you say that she's not patient? And now here you are, sharpening your machete. It's you who don't know what you're doing. She spends half her time helping you build your fortune and now, all of a sudden, you decide to go crazy."

"I'm not going crazy. She's the one who's betrayed me. She's supposed to be my wife but every day she goes off to laugh and play around with somebody else."

"That's how life in the market is. If you want to sell your stuff you have to smile and laugh. If you wanted her to stay at home you shouldn't have sent her out to work in the market in the first place. Okay. Let her stay home, but give her some children to look after. Then you can go out to the market. And besides, don't tell me that you don't have girlfriends tucked away in every corner of the village."

Muri smiled to himself as he thought about his servant's words. For years she'd been a good friend to the household, and she never said anything that didn't have a sound basis in fact.

If he and Ismiyati had had children things might not have turned out this way, with her getting lonely at home and deciding to work in the market. He would have been the one to go to market and to meet people from neighboring villages. He would be the one at whom customers smiled in hopes of obtaining a lower price. And no doubt, as well, he would have had female customers who found him attractive. In the end, he would have taken at least one of them for his next wife. Had he done that it wouldn't be he who was sharpening the machete, but Ismiyati who would be preparing to separate his neck from his body. Or she might curse him, or ask him for a divorce.... But if he didn't want to grant her a divorce then she would have to stay by his side and accept what caresses of his were left over from the other woman.

He laid the machete under the mango tree and watched his old servant as she straightened the *kebaya* and sash she always wore when she was going to pay a social call to a family celebrating an important event.

"Where are you off to?" he asked her.

"Out! I'm not going to stay around here with a crazy man."

"What's crazy about me?"

"What's not if you're planning to cut your wife's throat? The point is, I don't want to be a witness, because then I'd get called in by the police, too."

"Don't tell anyone, will you?"

"What do you mean, don't tell anyone? It's you who's got evil on your mind. Why should I keep my mouth shut? What, you think I'm supposed to be ashamed of not helping you? Is that it? You think that because you marry someone, that gives you the right to cut her throat? She's a person, too, and only God has the right to take a human life."

With that said, the servant left. On her way out the gate she glanced at Muri's machete lying on the ground beneath the mango tree and then gave him a scornful sneer.

Ismiyati usually came in by way of the gate near the mango tree. That was why he had left the machete there so as to be able to grab it quickly and use it to sever the graceful neck of the woman he expected to arrive home in just a few more minutes.

Muri smiled as he thought of what the servant had said. To himself he admitted the truth of her words. Ismiyati was indeed his wife but not his possession. Like everyone else she, too, belonged only to her heavenly creator. Muri was only her temporary caretaker. If he had wanted to take another wife Ismiyati would have let him, but he'd never suggested such a thing. If he had wanted to test his manhood with another woman, to see if he could produce children, Ismiyati would not have stood in his way. So why hadn't he? A hazy thought came to mind as he mused over the images of women he had managed to sleep with without his wife's ever finding out. None of them had ever gotten pregnant, he realized. He recalled how he had lost the fear of sleeping with any of the women who came to him in need of money and, thinking of this, he became aware that he himself was not as spotless as he might wish to be.

IT WAS WELL INTO THE NIGHT when Muri awoke from his nap and found Ismiyati sitting beside him, dressed in a sarong and a half-sewn blouse that she had just finished basting. She looked so much a nymph from heaven that at first he thought he must be dreaming. He rubbed his eyes several times to convince himself that what he saw was real. After he killed her, would she become a real heavenly nymph?

Noticing that he was awake, Ismiyati smiled sweetly at him. He saw that she held in her hands the machete that he'd sharpened that afternoon. She was still smiling as she whispered: "You're a good man, Muri. I was going to kill you because you haven't given me any children, but you've given me another kind of happiness."

Muri whispered back, "And you're a good woman, Ismiyati, because you have never left your husband, even though he's never given you any children."

Bursting into uproarious laughter, the two of them fell together onto the bed, where Muri's passionate embrace very soon caused the freshly basted seams of Ismiyati's blouse to break. Ismiyati's flawless skin made Muri soon forget what he had intended to do to the neck he kissed voraciously.

The rays of the morning sun sliced across the floor and into the bedroom whose door had been left unlocked the entire night. Muri and Ismiyati had also neglected to lock any of the other doors, so that when the servant arrived at the house her heart immediately began to pound. Her mind raced with questions. The open doors confirmed her worst fear: Muri had written the final chapter in his wife's life. Thus it was a great sense of relief that washed over her when she heard Ismiyati calling the name of her favorite kitten, Beggar. Her relief turned to joy when she saw that her employer was still among the living, with her head firmly attached to her neck.

"I'm off to the market," Ismiyati told the servant. "Cook something tasty for Pak Muri, will you? And let him sleep a little longer. He wants to stay in bed. He's tired from hunting last night."

"Hunting? What was he hunting?"

"Mosquitoes, of course. Why do you think his machete's lying over there in the corner?"

"His machete?"

Ismiyati smiled and went out the side door, going off to see all the friends who awaited her at the market.

Muri stretched out on the bed, wondering what in the world had made him cancel his intention of putting an end to his wife's life if it meant that she would go on leaving him alone each day. It must have been her eyes, or that face of hers that had made him forget about his well-sharpened machete. Or could it be true that she had a charm inserted between her eyes? The answer that came to him now seemed so clear that it made his head spin. He wanted to reach out for the hot coffee and the boiled eggs the servant had placed on the bedside table, but somehow he felt powerless, unable to move a muscle. All he felt was a mixture of paralysis, exhaustion, and anger.

1984

TRANSLATED BY THOMAS M. HUNTER

244

UMAR NUR ZAIN

Transaction

THE ROOM IS AIR-CONDITIONED, luxurious and done up in traditional decor. It's really a very pleasant place. None of those rude or bothersome young people who tend to look with suspicion on older people like me. And unlike the small clubs which abound in Jakarta, it's not filled with billows of smoke. Seated at the tables here are only foreigners, or rich people like myself.

The pretty women who work here are all outfitted in beautiful red batik costumes. They all know me. I often come here for dinner, to dispel the boredom of eating at home, where the menu is always the same. Here, dinner is 7,500 rupiah, and counting the cost of drinks and cigarettes, I end up spending only 10,000 rupiah altogether, a small amount compared to the daily expenditures of my household. I sip a drink the hotel calls an "Irian Mocha," while around me the pretty women, waiting on guests, hurry back and forth in their friendly way. When they walk, they sway. Their tight clothing makes their behinds pronounced, and their hips move as if following a beat. I draw deeply on my pipe. How nice life in Indonesia is now.

It's all thanks to development. Otherwise we certainly wouldn't be sitting here dressed in clean clothes, enjoying a lifestyle such as this. When my parents were still alive, all was suffering and war.

Fortunately God blessed my life and gave me the key position in the government that I now occupy. Money flows into my pockets like water. And not because of corruption, I'll have you know. It comes by itself. All I do is help my friends. There's nothing wrong with that, is there? And they show their appreciation with money. That's how things work in modern life.

Though when I look at some of my business contacts, the indigenous, Malay-blood ones especially, I can't help but think how stupid they are. I mean, when they come to me for help, do they ever think of the small details? After I've offered to help them all they can say is "thanks"; all I can do is take a deep breath and sigh. My Chinese contacts, on the other hand, are well aware of how things get done. Even without my asking, they come to the house and bring me things I need or money in large envelopes.

I can only say that those freedom fighters who dreamed of being teachers, lecturers, or civil servants after the revolution, yet who now refuse to take advantage of the opportunities presented them, are really quite ignorant. They waste their lives studying books, afraid of exploiting the opportunities that this age of development has provided. Well, if they like being poor, or if they're content to live in a shack, or out in some village, so be it. What do they expect?

The first floor show is starting. The girls who are to entertain us this evening with a program called "Evening in Paris" were brought in from France. A young man in a typically French costume appears alongside a kiosk that has been placed in the center of the stage. The lamp posts on stage look like they're straight out of France. The young Frenchman begins to play "I Love Paris" on his accordion. In a little while several sexy French girls appear and begin to dance gaily, occasionally giving a spirited hoot. Their smooth white thighs emerge from their short skirts, which are split almost up to the belly. Then, to give us an even more beautiful view, the girls take their skirts off altogether.

But unlike the shows in the more squalid clubs around town, the dancing here, though certainly sexy, is not in bad taste. These girls wear tight panties so that when they kick their legs high and shout hysterically, so typically French, they still present a most pleasing sight. And the floor show, even though it is a romantic tale of young lovers and includes a scene in bed, is not at all in bad taste. It may be erotic, but not excessively so.

I'm waiting for a woman by the name of Puspa. I don't know her very well but she has agreed to meet me here this evening, which is why I keep looking at the women who come into the club. Still the one I'm waiting for hasn't come. Already I've had to refuse, several times, the suggestions of the club's hostess that I begin my meal. Although my meeting here with Puspa is supposed to be of an erotic nature, there's an element of business in it, too. It's a unique transaction.

I draw again on my pipe. The thing appears almost to have gone out. Why is it that a man my age, fifty years old, is forever beset by physical temptation? Always the fire ready to flare up inside. This makes it very difficult for me to restrain myself in sexual matters; I simply can't keep women off my mind. Lucky for me, however, I have money, therefore plenty of opportunities to date pretty women. Though I'm not like some of my friends, other officials who keep a second or even a third wife on the sly. I prefer to take ordinary women to hotels without becoming involved in affairs.

Business relations of mine, especially the Chinese, who know of my proclivities used to take care of everything for me, sending pretty women directly to my office. But, in time, I grew tired of this. At my office I have a number of subordinates working together in a task force, ass kissers, yes, I know, but one needs employees of this sort who do whatever you want whenever you want it without thinking twice. Take my wife, for example. Let's say she needs an air conditioner for the car a business associate just gave me. Well, in the wink of an eye, there's my task-force. The next day – who knows how – the job's all taken care of. My wife's car is equipped with air conditioning.

247

This task force of mine also takes care of procuring female escorts for special guests and officials from the provinces, or wherever else. It was a member of the task force who first introduced me to Puspa, the woman who's supposed to meet me here.

Ah, there she is at last. The woman I've been waiting for, standing in the lobby. One of the waitresses escorts her to my table. She is beautiful with her hair falling neatly down her back, wearing a black gown, which contrasts nicely with her pale skin....

Her voice is soft and sweet. "Mr. Surya Kencana," she says. "Have you been waiting long?"

I stand. "It hasn't seemed long, because I was waiting for you."

The waitress pulls out a chair and Puspa takes her seat. "Sir, will you and Madame have your dinner now?" She opens a napkin and places it on Puspa's lap.

I order two snail soups as a starter.

WHILE EATING THE SOUP, I wonder at the strangeness of all this. I remember the other day when a member of my task force, the one who introduced me to Puspa, came to me with the suggestion of a new game. He knew a beautiful woman who was in need of money. Only 500,000 rupiah, he said. The money was needed for medical expenses; her child had something wrong with her eyes and needed to have an operation in Manila. Because she didn't know where to turn for the money and because the operation was needed soon, somehow she had gotten the idea of selling herself to me.

What's wrong with doing a good deed, I thought, especially if it means some new entertainment? I have the money and have to spend it somewhere. Nonetheless, I wanted to make sure that my subordinate was not trying to manipulate me – I wasn't going to be taken in too easily. High-class prostitutes use all sorts of tricks in their trade. Many would probably sell their own children.

"This is for real," my subordinate insisted. "She's a modern girl.

Her only problem is that she married too young and has a husband. But she's never sold herself before or had affairs like others."

There seemed no reason for him to lie; I had, after all, only recently given him a promotion. But because it was a new game, I wanted to make sure he was telling me the truth. Nobody wants to throw away that much money just to find himself with some run-of-the-mill, high-class prostitute. Even a famous high-class call girl wouldn't cost 500,000 rupiah.

When Puspa was introduced to me several days later at the office, I was extremely impressed. She was pretty, a very good-looking woman, and she really did give me the impression of being a modern girl, dressed fashionably, with makeup on. A little coy. At the same time, I also felt that she really had tried to be a good wife and that her failure was the result of matters quite outside her control. But, living in this modern and materialistic world, she was able to see that she still had a final option. She had her body, after all. Nevertheless my instinct for caution told me to check her out further, to see whether or not her story was true.

Somewhat embarrassed, but steadfast, Puspa invited me to her home to ascertain the facts for myself. "But please pretend you're just an ordinary older man," she said, "because I told my husband that I was going to borrow the money we need from my office, through official channels."

I went that evening to Puspa's house. After my driver parked the car, I walked down a narrow side street. Her house was not as simple as those around it, though it was certainly far from anything like the grand homes that line Jakarta's major boulevards.

Her husband and child were at home. As an official I have a great deal of practice in acting out roles. I know when to be angry, when to be polite and patient, when to defer to higher-ranking officials, and when to act like a big shot, or simply a model, blameless official. I can put on whatever face the situation requires.

249

Puspa's husband, I learned, was a member of a not-so-famous band. He had a contract with a small nightclub but, because the club kept losing customers, his earnings were minimal. I noticed on a side stand an enlarged photograph of the young husband with his wife and their child. They were a handsome family, a new generation with a bright future. It was somewhat difficult for me to reconcile this thought with Puspa's decision. Had fate so altered their future? Maybe Puspa's love for her daughter had made her decision an easy one. I could imagine how difficult it would be for her to come up with the 500,000 rupiah she needed in so short a time. The situation had required an extraordinary response.

I looked at her daughter, thin and weak, sitting on a chair. She wore thick glasses and in fact looked to be very much in need of help. I approached the little girl like a doctor and, who knows, maybe she thought I was a doctor. I told her to take off her glasses. Then I took hold of her eyelashes and pulled her lids upward to expose her eyeballs. Even I could see that the girl was in critical need of help.

"Yes, I'm afraid that your girl does need medical help, and fast," I said as I put the thick glasses back on the girl's nose. I stroked her hair and for fully another half hour acted the role of a doctor, all the while with Puspa's husband having no idea of what I was going to receive in return for my money.

NOW, IN THE CLUB, the French dance number begins to heat up. I watch one of the women dance erotically beneath the lights of Paris, her desire making her writhe like a cat. I fondled Puspa's arm, then squeeze her smooth fingers. For her this may be the first time she's done such a thing with a man other than her husband. But what business is that of mine?

We eat our dinners in a relaxed manner, taking our time with the steaks I've ordered. The wine is sweet and strong. I begin to feel lightheaded. A warm feeling spreads through my body.

After the meal I suggest we leave the club. I sign the check and leave a tip, and Puspa takes her handbag and follows me. As we walk down the corridor of the hotel and enter the elevator that will take us to the sixth floor, the eyes of many of the men watching us seem to show resentment. What's a man of my age doing holding the hand of Puspa, a woman in her twenties?

At the room I open the door and motion for Puspa to come in. "Here?" she asks, almost inaudibly, her eyes surveying the room. She moves listlessly, hesitant, but enters. I whistle cheerfully as I disrobe. I take a housecoat from my overnight bag and look in the mirror: my hair is starting to turn white and my skin shows more wrinkles, but my eyes are still bright. I don't feel close to my age at all!

I look at Puspa, sitting in her black gown on the edge of the bed. She is a goddess – elegant and smooth-skinned, with a body worthy of adoration. I wash my face and comb my hair, then go to Puspa. I sit down beside her. I touch her shoulders and kiss her temples. I hear my own breath coming faster.

Puspa's throat trembles as she tries to control her voice. "What should I do?"

"Undress," I whisper.

Puspa stands and slowly opens the zipper on the back of her dress. The black gown falls to the floor in a heap.

The room's television is on. Now it's Henny Purwonegoro, in a program too-often interrupted by commercials. Henny sings energetically; she wears tight slacks and a stretch top. Her oval face looks very pretty indeed.

"Now what?" Puspa asks, even more softly. There's almost no strength in her voice.

"Everything," I tell her.

Puspa places her arms behind her head.

I hear Kris Biantoro interviewing ladies who praise a soap they've just tried for the first time.

"Now what?" She's almost crying.

I don't answer her. The bed is beautifully done with a reddish-orange spread and brilliant white sheets. This hotel's management certainly knows how to create a romantic atmosphere. I move toward Puspa. She loosens her hair while staring at me. Her eyes glisten. Her lips begin to part.

I hear on the television a lively, spirited, number. I think it must be Ervina, a Javanese singer who always wears brown pants and likes to twist and turn when singing popular songs.

THE NEXT MORNING I awake refreshed. I whistle as I go into the bathroom. A good shower with warm water is very invigorating. I feel like a young man again. I turn off the shower, rub myself dry with the towel, and after putting on my housecoat I go to the window of my sixth-floor room.

I open it. The day is clear and bright. Below, the smooth asphalt streets are jammed with luxury cars. The city stretches far away beneath me and I think of how much I enjoy modern-day Jakarta.

In the distance, on the other side of a filthy, black river full of garbage, I can see small huts that remind me of snail shells. Even from this distance I can see that the occupants are dressed in rumpled clothes. I really can't understand poor people at all. They work all day and all night, just to put a little money aside for food. Busting their asses. No, they really don't deserve the right to enjoy life in a luxury hotel, let alone to sleep with a beautiful woman like Puspa!

I take a deep breath and take stock in the mirror, examining my face with its wrinkles and white hair. I draw a breath of elation and victory. I feel proud. I'm a good and generous official. This day I helped a child who's nearly blind.

1982

TRANSLATED BY MILDRED L. E. WAGEMANN

Contributors' Notes

AHMAD TOHARI, born in 1948 in Tanggarjaya near Banyumas, Central Java, has been editor of the family magazine *Amanah* since 1986. **B.Y. TAND**, who was born in Indrapura, Asahan (North Sumatra) in 1942, works for the Department of Education and Culture. BUDI DARMA, born in Rembang, Central Java, in 1937 is a lecturer at the Surabaya Teachers' College. CHAIRIL ANWAR was born in Medan, Sumatra, in 1922. He died in 1949. DANARTO, born in Mojowetan, Central Java, in 1940, has taught at at the Jakarta Arts Institute since 1973. GERSON POYK, born in Namodale, Roti (Timor), in 1931 is one of Indonesia's most prolific writers. HAMSAD RANGKUTI, born in Titikuning near Medan, North Sumatra, in 1943 is the editor of *Horison*. J.E. SIAHAAN was born in Balige, North Sumatra, in 1934. LEILA S. CHUDORI, born in 1962 in Jakarta, is a reporter for *Tempo* news magazine. LINUS SURYADI was born in Yogyakarta in 1951. A member of the Yogyakarta Arts Council, since 1986 he has been editor of *Citra Yogya*. NH. DINI, born in Semarang, Central Java, in 1936 spends most of her time writing and taking care of the library she established in her home city. PUTU WIJAYA, who was born in Tabanan, Bali, in 1944 enjoys a busy life as a journalist, writer and theater and film director. SAPARDI DJOKO DAMONO, who was born in Solo, Central Java, in 1940 is currently the assistant rector of the Faculty of Letters at the University of Indonesia. SENO GUMIRA AJIDARMA, who is also known by the name of Mira Sato, is an editor of popular news weekly *Jakarta-Jakarta*. He was born in Boston, the United States, in 1958. SITOR SITUMORANG was born in Harianboho, North Sumatra, in 1924. He now resides in the Netherlands. SUBAGIO

SASTROWARDOYO was born near the city of Madiun, East Java, in 1924. He works for the state publishing house Balai Pustaka. SUTARDJI CALZOUM BACHRI was born in 1941 in Rengat, Riau. Very active in Jakarta's art circles, he has served as editor of *Horison* since 1979. TITIS BASINO, a frequent contributor to magazines and journals, was born in Magelang, Central Java, in 1939. UMAR NUR ZAIN was born in 1939 in Cirebon, Central Java. He is now one of the senior editors at *Suara Pembaruan*, a Jakarta daily. YUDHI SOERJOATMODJO, born in Jakarta in 1964, works as a photographer and journalist for *Tempo*.

MARGARET GLADE AGUSTA is the editorial and language consultant for *Jakarta Post*, a Jakarta daily. DESI ANWAR works at RCTI, Indonesia's first private television company. T.E. BEHREND is working on a manuscript conservation project at the National Library of Indonesia. MARC BENAMOU is currently doing his doctoral research in ethnomusicology in Surkarta, Central Java. ALAN FEINSTEIN is the Cultural Affairs Officer for The Ford Foundation. THOMAS HUNTER, the translator of *The Weaverbirds*, another Lontar publication, is the director of the School for International Training in Bali. JENNIFER LINDSAY is the Cultural Affairs Officer for the Australian embassy. JOHN H. MCGLYNN is the vice chairman and editor of The Lontar Foundation. EDMUND EDWARDS MCKINNON is currently assisting the National Research Institute of Archeology and the Directorate for the Preservation of Cultural Heritage in assembling a database inventory of archeological sites, photgraphs, drawings and maps. MARY LOU WANG, an Indonesian-born American, lives and works in New Jersey. D.M. ROSKIES teaches at the University of Papua Niugini. CLAIRE SIVERSON is currently pursuing a graduate degree in clinical social work at Smith College in Northampton, Massachusettes. TOENGGOEL P. SIAGIAN is the executive director of the Jakarta Christian School Association. MILDRED L.E. WAGEMANN, a free lance writer and translator, resides in Jakarta.

Credits & Sources

SHORT STORIES:

Minem Has a Baby (*Si Minem Beranak Bayi*): from *Senyum Karyamin*, Gramedia, Jakarta, 1989. **Zero Point** (*Titik Nol*): from *Horison*, Vol. XVII, No. 9, 1982. **Orez**: from *Orang-Orang Bloomington*, Sinar Harapan, Jakarta, 1980. **Mother's Wall** (*Dinding Ibu*): from *Berhala*, Pustaka Firdaus, Jakarta, 1987. **Matias Akankari**: from *Matias Akankari*, Balai Pustaka, Jakarta, 1975. **The Fence** (*Pagar*): from *Horison*, Vol. XVIII, No. 4, 1983. This translation first appeared in somewhat different form in *Manoa* (Vol. 3 No. 1), University of Hawaii. **When the Rain Falls** (*Jika Hujan Turun*): from *Kisah*, Vol. IV, No. 10, October 1956. **Paris, June 1988** (*Paris, Juni 1988*): from *Malam Terakhir*, Grafiti Pers, Jakarta, 1988. **The Purification of Sita** (*Air Suci Sita*): from *Malam Terakhir*, Grafiti Pers, Jakarta, 1988. This translation first appeared in somewhat different form in *Solidarity* (No. 123, July-September 1989), Manila. **Broken Wings** (*Jatayu*): from *Dua Dunia*, NV Nusantara, Bukit Tinggi & Jakarta, 1956, reprinted in *Liar*, Nur Cahaya, Yogyakarta, 1989. **Blood** (*Darah*): from Horison, Vol. XXII, August 1987. This translation first appeared in somewhat different form in *Manoa* (Vol. 3 No. 1). **The Gift** (*Hadiah*): from *Gres*, Balai Pustaka, Jakarta, 1982. **The River's Song** (*Nyanyian Sepanjang Sungai*): from *Manusia Kamar dan 14 Cerpen Lainnya*, Haji Masagung, Jakarta, 1988. This translation first appeared in somewhat different form in *Manoa* (Vol. 3 No. 1). **Jinn** (*Djin*): from *Konfrontasi*, March-April (No. 5), 1955. **Holy Communion** (*Perjamuan Kudus*): from *Danau Toba*, Dunia Pustaka Jaya, Jakarta, 1981. This translation first appeared in somewhat different form in *Manoa*

(Vol. 3 No. 1). **The Charm** (*Susuk*): from *Horison*, Vol. XVIII, No. 3, March 1984. **Warsiah** (*Janda Muda*): from *Segi dan Garis*, Dunia Pustaka Jaya, Jakarta, 1983. **Transaction** (*Transaksi*): from *Horison*, Vol. XVII, Nos. 3-4, March-April, 1982. This translation first appeared in somewhat different form in *Manoa* (Vol. 3 No. 1).

POETRY:

CHAIRIL ANWAR: Pines in the Distance (*Derai-Derai Cemara*), My Friend and I (*Kawanku dan Aku*) from *Kerikil Tajam dan Yang Terampas dan Yang Putus*), Dian Rakyat, Jakarta, 1985 (9th Printing); No, Woman! (Original is untitled) and Announcement (*Pemberian Tahu*) from *The Complete Poems of Chairil Anwar*, Liaw Yock-Fang/H.B. Jassin, University Education Press, Singapore, 1974. SAPARDI DJOKO DAMONO: All poems from *Mata Pisau*, Bandung, 1974, later reprinted by Balai Pustaka, Jakarta, 1982. SITOR SITUMORANG: Cathèdral de Chartres and Poem (*Sajak*) from *Surat Kertas Hijau*, Dian Rakyat, Jakarta, 1953; La Ronde, I, Morning Field (*Lapangan Pagi*) and Pilgrimage to a Mountain Church (*Ziarah dalam Gereja Gunung*) from *Wajah Tak Bernama*, Jakarta, 1955. SUTARDJI CALZOUM BACHRI: All poems from *O Amuk Kapak*, Sinar Harapan, Jakarta, 1981.
Translations of all poems by John H. McGlynn.

OTHERS:

"Philosophy & Poetry," by Subagio Sastrowardoyo, originally titled "Filsafat dan Puisi Modern Indonesia," from *Pengarang Modern Sebagai Manusia Perbatasan*, Balai Pustaka, Jakarta, 1989.

Excerpts of Pariyem's Confession by Linus Suryadi taken from *Pengakuan Pariyem*, Sinar Harapan, Jakarta, 1981.

"*Labyrinth*," the painting used for the cover of this volume, reproduced by the kind permission of the artist.

Contributions to Indonesian Literature in Translation

The Lontar Foundation is a non-profit organization whose aims are fostering greater appreciation of Indonesian literature and culture, supporting the work of authors and translators of Indonesian literature, and improving the quality of publication and distribution of Indonesian literary works and translations. Previous publications include:

Shadows on the Silver Screen,
a social history of Indonesian film by Salim Said;
Golden Letters : Writing Tranditions of Indonesia,
a catalogue of Indonesian mansucripts from British collections, by
Annabel T. Gallup and Ben Arps;
The Weaverbirds,
a novel by Y.B. Mangunwijaya;
On Foreign Shores: American Images in Indonesian Poetry;
Walking Westward in the Morning:
Seven Contemporary Indonesian Poets;
Shackles,
a novel by Armijn Pane; and
Suddenly the Night,
an anthology of poetry by Sapardi Djoko Damono.

For more information about the Lontar Foundation and its activities please write to:
Jl. Danau Maninjau No. 93, Pejompongan, Jakarta 10210.